Praise for

FEEL THE ROCK

"This is gold. You will laugh, smile, cry, and take a dozen trips down memory lane(s).

"For anyone who has ever traveled in developing regions, for anyone who has traveled solo, and certainly for those who have traveled in Bolivia, this is a must read. Lou captures the sights, culture, experiences, smells, sounds, and true feel of being in a foreign land so adeptly that he evokes notions and memories that were otherwise buried or thought to be long gone. So often people romanticize travel and tell only the positive stories, sharing only the beautiful photos from tops of mountains and smiling groups of children enthralled by a funny looking foreigner, but rarely do we get pulled back into the real "feels" of solo travel; the hardships, the loneliness, the second-guessing, the fear and anxiety of being truly alone and lost even when surrounded by millions of people…and the stuff in our lives responsible for pulling us out of those low places, family, friends, and faith."

—MICHELLE ZIMMERMAN, Co-Founder, Pidola

Feel the Rock

by Lou Fabian

© Copyright 2024 Lou Fabian

ISBN 979-8-88824-417-3

All rights reserved. No part of this publication may be reproduced, stored in a retrieval system, or transmitted in any form or by any means—electronic, mechanical, photocopy, recording, or any other—except for brief quotations in printed reviews, without the prior written permission of the author.

Published by

3705 Shore Drive
Virginia Beach, VA 23455
800-435-4811
www.koehlerbooks.com

FEEL THE ROCK

FEEL THE ROCK

LOU FABIAN

VIRGINIA BEACH
CAPE CHARLES

DEDICATION

I'd like to dedicate this book to both my parents, because without their support and guidance, I'm not the person I am today... love you guys.

PREFACE

My friends and I have a saying when we would go rock climbing and bad weather was forecasted— "feel the rock." Instead of just canceling plans, we would always head out to the crag to feel the rock before deciding. If the rock was wet, we would grab food instead. If the rock was dry, we would climb. No decisions about climbing were made until we felt the rock first, until we understood what we'd be dealing with.

What if we didn't make major decisions in life until we felt the rock inside ourselves, to understand who we really are? To understand what makes us think and behave the way we do? The true you, before all the conditioning, negative muscle memory, all the bullshit? But first, we have to find the courage to lean and look into places that scare us the most. It's crazy that we'll do almost anything to *not* look; it's just too painful.

• • •

What follows is the story of my years in Bolivia, told in the third person. It is an account of my attempt to "find the rock" in my own life. Most names have been changed, but the experiences and locations portrayed here are true. Dialogue has been created to best capture the mood and discourse between the book's main characters, and scenes have been enhanced or abbreviated for continuity, consistency, and readability.

It would be impossible to reconstruct verbatim every conversation and adventure undertaken during my time in South America. So, I focused on the highlights and aspects of my journey that I felt were most relevant and interesting, and I tell them through the perspective of my protagonist, Gabe.

So, in truth, what you're about to read is a fictionalized memoir told in the third person where I take liberty to make these adventures entertaining and accessible. At the end of this book, you'll see a first-person postface explaining how this book came into existence and my journey as an author. Enjoy!

CHAPTER ONE
THE EXTORTIONIST

Gabe stared out of the van at the thick smog. The choking gray layer in the atmosphere matched the inside of his head; he was in a serious daze. The fog of jet lag and the exhaustion of trying to recover from eighteen-plus hours of travel were making it nearly impossible for him to see straight.

It was his first time in Cochabamba, a city in central Bolivia that sits in a bowl surrounded by mountains. There's no place for exhaust and trash-burn smoke to escape, and it gets especially unbearable in the dry season. So when Gabe and the others in his group made their way to the hotel from the airport, it was hard for them to breathe, never mind see. Despite the foul air their spirits remained buoyed by the volunteer work they'd come here to do.

So far, for most of the group, arriving had been without major incident. After landing in La Paz, they'd collected their bags, met their liaison, grabbed breakfast, guzzled lots of coffee to combat the jet lag, then leaped into the final leg of the trip, the short flight to Cochabamba, one hundred and eighty miles southeast of La Paz.

For a thirty-six-year-old, Gabe had traveled quite a bit and knew how fortunate he was for the experiences. In fact, he assured friends he was totally aware of being born on second base. Or, for football fans, on the fifty -yard line. He was cognizant of his privilege and grateful for a good education and a family that valued learning about other people and cultures.

But Gabe had never been to South America. Even knowing all that, he was about to get a huge reality check as Bolivia is the second poorest country in the Western Hemisphere. In 2015, only Haiti had a lower standard of living. There for a week with a group from his church in Golden, Colorado, he was about to see conditions unlike anything he'd experienced.

• • •

As Gabe had grown older, he'd become less comfortable flying. Something about coming in for landings made him queasy—even nauseated. On the flight, as the other members of the group yammered about who knows what, Gabe was doing everything he knew to keep from throwing up. His clothes, his headrest, and even his seat had ended up soaked with sweat.

Sure, Gabe had experienced discomfort on flights lately, but typically he recovered soon after landing. Not this time.

La Paz provided some unique physical demands the moment he stepped off the plane. First was the altitude. El Alto, the city where La Paz's airport is located, sits at 13,000 feet above sea level—one of the highest airports in the world. Even coming in from Colorado, he struggled. He couldn't catch a deep breath, resulting in a dreaded altitude headache the instant he got off the plane. Being at a high altitude can cause your head to swell, which is what was happening. He could feel the pressure building behind his eyes and took a small dosage of Tylenol.

Another detail of the La Paz airport is that—in 2015 at least—it lacked the modern infrastructure Westerners take for granted. The jetway provided little protection from the outside elements. It was winter there when the group arrived, and due to the higher altitude, the freezing air permeating the jetway walls practically froze Gabe's clothing to his skin. It wouldn't have been as bad, and he wouldn't have minded as much, if his clothes weren't sweat soaked, and if he hadn't absentmindedly packed his cold-weather travel gear in his checked suitcase. Packing mistake number one.

So, Gabe's first ten minutes in Bolivia included shortness of breath, nausea, headache, and chills added to drowsiness from the long trip.

Good times, Gabe thought, but kept right on rolling.

Blindly, wondering when his pain killer would finally kick in, Gabe had followed the crowd through various drab concrete walkways until finally reaching customs and passport control, where the uncomfortableness continued. The customs agent looked him up and down and said, "*Trescientos dólores.*" Three hundred dollars.

"*Como?*" Gabe asked.

"*Trescientos dólores,*" the agent repeated.

"*What?*" he asked, still doing everything he could to not throw up, in this case and quite literally, right onto the customs agent. "*Como?*"

"*Trescientos dólores.*"

They were getting nowhere fast. Even though Gabe's Spanish was limited, he knew something wasn't right. He'd read that tourist visas cost one hundred and sixty-five dollars. He'd also heard that some customs officials liked to ask for more, but nearly double. Ugh, total extortion. But it didn't look like he had any choice. He forked it over.

Those first few minutes in Bolivia in 2015 foreshadowed pretty much all of Gabe's subsequent visits to the country. He learned something that day and during the week after that he would retain for good: *You are never really comfortable in Bolivia.* It could be physical discomfort, embarrassing cultural misunderstandings, the frustration of not being able to communicate, the realistic threat of a kidnapping, or a maze of all of the above in which he became nearly irreparably lost. There was *always* something that kept him out of his comfort zone.

But no growth happens in your comfort zone.

CHAPTER TWO
BEARDED DIPLOMACY

The next morning when waking up with the group in Cochabamba, Gabe felt like he was shot out of a cannon. He was excited to get started on the group's two primary projects: helping to distribute iron supplements to local schoolchildren and assisting in the building of a nearby church. Lots to get accomplished in seven days.

After breakfast, they met people from a partner organization, Food for the Hungry, who would act as liaisons and project coordinators. They were all Bolivianos and Cochabambinos, all fully and faithfully committed to the work they were doing. After all, the projects were within their own neighborhoods and communities, and they lived and breathed them daily. One who impressed Gabe right away as being kind and friendly was Alejandra, Ali for short, who spoke near-perfect English.

The first order of business was a visit to a school south of the Cochabamba in one of the newly developing suburbs called Monte Rancho. But as the van neared the area, there was nothing even remotely similar to American suburbs—no McMansions or cul-de-sacs, not even paved roads. Gabe and the group were in the midst of squatter towns with small houses constructed of mud bricks.

A local family—parents and their four kids, all under age ten—had lunch prepared and ready for the group. The family was sponsored by a couple from Gabe's church back in Colorado, which had provided funds to help this Cochabambino family with school supplies and basic household items. Because many of the families either had only one income—almost always the father's—or none at all, they needed assistance wherever they could find it. One of the first things that impressed Gabe when visiting this individual family for lunch was the general lack of everything that he almost always took for granted back home in the US.

It was heartbreaking for Gabe, his first in-person exposure to abject poverty. Rotten living conditions; a family with no bathroom, just one bedroom for all six family members, a small kitchen with a gas range, and no running water. On later trips all throughout Bolivia, Gabe would see even worse, but this was difficult and humbling to witness; his face revealed his anguish and surprise. Despite the family's limited resources, they welcomed the Americans warmly. They had prepared an excellent lunch of chicken, quinoa, and soup. Gabe came to learn that lunch—and this particular fare—is a major meal in Bolivian culture, and a central focus of the day. For this family to host the group and provide what was for them a significant meal was a massive gesture. It was an introduction to the level of hospitality that Gabe would experience all throughout the country. No matter how poor the families he visited he rarely left hungry.

After lunch, the group headed to the local school to distribute iron tablets to the schoolchildren. Of all the buildings and infrastructure in the area, the school was by far the most developed, comprised of a handful of concrete buildings where the school rooms were located. The "campus" accommodated every grade, so about a thousand kids of all ages were roaming the grounds. There was also the ubiquitous soccer field. Soccer is close to religion all over Latin America, and Bolivia is no different. Occasionally, you'd find a school soccer field that was even covered to accommodate matches in all weather, and this school had one of those.

A half dozen lines of the hundreds of students stood on the open-air soccer field. Gabe took his place at the head of one line; just behind him was a table covered with iron tablets. He was a bit anxious about how it was all going to transpire. As he started handing the tablets out, the kids looked at him curiously. You could see in their faces that they were asking themselves, *Who the hell is this guy?* Naturally, the group of Americans stuck out. But then Gabe realized that it was his beard that had these kids fascinated. He'd been growing it out for close to a year, and it was hanging down to his chest. Bolivian men don't have much facial hair, so to them Gabe must have looked like he was from another planet. Gabe was surely a novelty, probably even an oddity, to all these kids.

There are many different types of diplomacy across the world: cultural, public, economic, etc. Gabe seemed to have established a new type—bearded diplomacy. Given that Gabe was now an unofficial ambassador to them, he took responsibility for the interactions they were having. There was a strong chance that he was the first American they had ever met. He quickly discovered that the best act of statesmanship was to let the smaller kids interact with *la barba*. At first, they would just come up and give it a quick feel, the way someone would approach an unknown dog. Then after a quick pet, they'd give a bit of a tug. After a tug, there would be a full-on pull; some ended up nearly hanging from his facial hair. All it took was for one kid to try and the others would gather around for a tug as well. It was as if the children weren't lined up to receive the iron tablets anymore, but to yank the strange looking guy's facial hair.

Handing out the iron tablets led to another of Gabe's early realizations of how scarce resources were in Bolivia, and particularly in these squatter towns. In most Western countries, iron is in the daily diet, so most people tend not to give it much thought. Gabe certainly never had. But in communities that lack a varied, healthy diet, iron deficiency could cause both physical and mental stunted growth, especially for school-aged children.

Gabe wasn't aware of this issue going into the project, but that day, the group's coordinators educated them. Iron is critical to childhood development, and these kids needed it through the supplements the group was handing out.

The interactions with, and reactions from, the schoolchildren were priceless, a once-in-a-lifetime experience. The interactions followed a pattern; first curiosity, then a growing comfort level, then true interaction and enjoyment of his facial hair as a novelty, then finally "acceptance" of him. Gabe was a person, too! These precious moments were exactly why Gabe had wanted to travel with his church group.

After distributing the iron tablets for a couple of hours, the group moved to a public soccer field to give each local child a toothbrush and toothpaste. It was again eye-opening to see that the group needed to teach many of the children how to use these basic hygiene tools. It wasn't just a lack of the needed specific resources and items. What was lacking was much more significant.

Through coordinators and interpreters, the group showed the kids how to put paste on the brush, wet the brush, brush in circles, rinse, and repeat by demonstrating it firsthand, and then helping them with their own teeth. There was also the educational component of why this twice-a-day exercise was so important. It was shocking to Gabe that these children didn't know how important it was to take care of their teeth. And they weren't toddlers; they were five, six, maybe eight years old.

For the second time that day, he was surprised and humbled by the poverty and lack of resources in these communities. Gabe also felt happy he could make a small, positive impact on the kids' lives.

• • •

The group ended the day at the Food for the Hungry offices in Cochabamba. It was the chance to debrief as a group and digest the day's activities. About twenty people sat around a large wooden table and one by one stood to share what had impacted them the most. One after another, they testified to how lasting the memories of the day's activities were surely going to be. One member of the delegation echoed Gabe's feelings about how interactions with the schoolchildren would stay with them forever.

The most profound impression Gabe gleaned came from the family who had served the church volunteer's lunch. While he was there, he kept thinking to himself, *How is this family even making ends meet on a daily basis?* Sure, they had their sponsorship money coming in, but what if they didn't have that source of income? They were in dire straits as it was, but it could have been worse. The strength of this family seemed otherworldly and left him feeling guilty. What he complained about at home now felt trivial. He felt ashamed and in awe of the grace and humility the Bolivian family had showed.

The last person to speak at the debriefing was a short (probably about five feet tall), stout Bolivian man named Felix, the director for the greater team of coordinators. Gabe was once again awed. This man had four children of his own and yet had adopted four more children after one of his siblings died. Seemingly everyone had a big heart, one bigger than the next.

Felix spoke in Spanish, so Gabe didn't catch what he had found most memorable that day. But anyone could see how touched Felix was and how much he appreciated the group's work. Whatever it was he said, he shared through tears. Gabe instantly understood how important their small contributions were to the growth of this community. Felix was tireless and his work endless, and yet he appreciated the group's help. To Gabe, it was inspiring.

The following days were full of visits sprinkled in and around Cochabamba. One afternoon they visited an educational center to learn more about Bolivian culture. Another day they hiked up a local peak called Cerro Tunari. These activities not only helped to balance the overall experience of visiting this new country, but also to teach the group about a day-in-the-life of a Bolivian. The primary goals of the trip were to help support these projects, of course, but secondary was to also immerse the American volunteers in the culture. Gabe saw firsthand how a variety of people in this poor country lived. It was knowledge he would carry back to Colorado, knowledge that was unknowingly going to change his future.

• • •

On the group's last full day in South America, they returned to the squatter town of Monte Rancho for the construction of a church. The vision of the church was modest—a two-room structure with walls made of mud and brick similar to the homes of those it would serve. As they drove up to the location, they could see there wasn't much of a structure. There wasn't much of anything other than the concrete floor, some water drainage ditches surrounding the foundation, and piles of rock and brick scattered around. There was dust in the air, as it hadn't rained for the previous few weeks. The group was welcomed not only by the church's managers and engineers, but by the local cats, dogs, and cows that freely roamed the neighborhood.

The task for that day was to move rocks and bricks from one place to another, essentially to stage the construction of the side and back walls. Any activities that involved engineering skills were going to be completely outside of their little group.

That day, the Coloradans were just a human-powered component of the larger operation. They started early in the morning and worked hard and diligently for a solid six or seven hours. It was clear that everyone wanted to show good old American work ethic in action, so the group rolled up their proverbial sleeves and immersed in the effort. It was exhausting and everyone was soaked in sweat. Yet, at the end of the day, they hadn't even made a dent in the pile, even with all of them moving at an almost frenetic pace. So much more needed to be done, but the group was hopeful that they had at least shortened the time to get the church up and running for the community. Leaving the work incomplete bothered Gabe. He wished he could have done more.

While they were moving the materials from place to place, the church leaders educated the Americans on how tremendously important religion—primarily Christianity—and the church are to Bolivians. Of course, religion is important to people all over the world, but for people who live in poverty, with next to nothing, religion is vital to keep hope alive. In underserved communities all over the world, families depend on religion to sustain them, and look to churches as a gel for their communities. Gabe was witnessing that in Monte Rancho.

He then started to realize that poverty takes various shapes and sizes and is multidimensional. Things like a house, a car, a boat, and an education all that come with the Western style of living, signify that someone is wealthy and successful. Sure, huge swaths of American kids also lack those things, but running water, electricity, and an indoor toilet? Almost everyone in the US has these things, and yet a significant percentage of Bolivians did not. However, Gabe would observe that they are rich in other ways. Like in faith, family bonds, and community. How many people of the twenty-first century can honestly say they have those? It made Gabe realize that anyone can have some form of poverty in their lives, regardless of background and upbringing. Including him. At the top of the list? No family of his own yet. Also, no real, meaningful purpose.

• • •

Riding back to the hotel, Gabe thought about how in general, lack of community and disconnection within families in the US would seem utterly crazy to Bolivians. It struck him as ironic that those with so much less material wealth and creature comforts would feel sorry for *him*.

Gabe was only seven days into his first trip to South America, seven productive, incredible days. A week of memories, stories, and experiences that would last him a lifetime. He met people who left a profound impression on him; he assisted in work that filled his heart; he explored a part of himself that was new and would become part of his core. He just didn't know it yet.

His journey to find meaning had begun, but he had no idea how long it would be or how many twists and turns it would entail. Life can't be scripted.

CHAPTER THREE
PEOPLE DO CARE

Back in Colorado after his initial trip to Bolivia in 2015, Gabe's girlfriend, Anna, wanted to hear every detail. He'd been back a few days when they finally had a chance to connect in person. He found that he had so much to tell that he couldn't share it all fast enough, hoping not to leave anything out.

"That first day after arriving, I was so excited to get started . . . we all were," he said. "We were pumped and ready to go." His mind was racing.

Anna of course already knew what the group's main goals had been with the iron tablets and the church construction. But he wanted to tell her not just the details of what he'd seen, what the people he met were like, what he'd learned about the culture and the poverty, but also about some of the emotions that were sparked.

Gabe told her about the trip coordinators who had met them and how committed they were to making the trip a success. "They lived and breathed these projects," he said. "Considering how positively they affected their neighborhoods and communities, you can see why. It was impressive how much they simply just . . . cared."

Anna listened intently, and Gabe was grateful for that. He told her about the village they visited south of Cochabamba. "They're not suburbs like in Denver," he said. "They seemed more like squatter towns. In Monte Rancho, the houses and other buildings looked like they'd just sprung up overnight. There was nothing like we have here—no paved roads, no services, no police, no nothing. There wasn't even electricity. The nights were pitch black. No street lamps."

"Crazy," Anna said, smiling. "But I bet the people were happier than most of us here."

Gabe smiled back, remembering. "Yep. They have one another. That's the most important thing to them—community and family." How different they'd been from the people he and Anna came in contact with regularly. "They were moving into these towns so fast the government can't keep up with them," Gabe added. "Although I think even if they could, the government couldn't afford to build all that infrastructure that's needed. But still the Bolivianos who live in rural areas move closer to cities because they need work. It's like the reverse of here, where people leave cities to get space between them and everyone else."

Gabe went on to tell her how impressed he was with the family and neighborhood they visited on that first day. "Some families had satellite TV dishes on the sides of their houses, which was either an expression of optimism or just for show, since there was no power to the house."

Gabe was still a bit jet lagged but so energized from his experiences that he felt like he could talk all night. When he told Anna about giving out the tablets, she smiled. "I think I was the first American they'd ever seen. And this beard—" He tugged on it.

Anna laughed. "Even here, your beard is . . . *awesome*."

For a moment, there was a comfortable silence. Then Gabe said, "The whole experience is a perfect example of how people who do good work get more back than what they give."

"Will you go back?" Anna asked.

Gabe didn't even pause to think. "I don't think so. There are so many other places I want to go and experience. But I'll continue to do the service here in town. It was an amazing feeling watching the look in those kids' eyes. And I think about showing them how to brush their teeth for the very first time. It's incredible how something so small can feel so meaningful, whereas we go days, months, maybe years here without getting that feeling."

Anna narrowed her eyes but said nothing.

Gabe was right; helping others had set something in motion within him. But about not going back to Bolivia? Gabe couldn't have been more wrong.

CHAPTER FOUR
MOVING OUT WEST

Gabe had moved around the US a bit in his twenties and early thirties and ended up in Colorado almost by chance. One night over a couple of beers with John, a friend, while in Charleston, South Carolina back in 2009, small talk took on some depth. John and he got into some personal topics—rare for Gabe—specifically how he was struggling with his place and role at work and feeling uncomfortable.

Gabe had been employed by a small advertising agency, and the work was mostly okay. An old boss had hired him to establish a new department and spearhead some new projects within the agency, but shortly after Gabe had arrived, the old boss had left, which made him feel uncertain about the entire endeavor. He'd moved five hundred miles for this new job, and his future was now a bit uncertain.

"Gabe, you can do what you do anywhere," John had encouraged. "Have you thought about what you want to do with your time *outside* of work?"

Gabe didn't have an answer. Then something was triggered inside Gabe. "I want to be closer to the mountains."

John raised an eyebrow and then asked, "Where the hell did that come from?"

Gabe had visited his extended family in Colorado years before, and the mountains had, deep down, left their mark. But he hadn't planned to move there until that very moment, that very instant. It never even crossed his mind. Suddenly, Gabe could clearly see his path. He was convinced that he needed a change, not just something new at work. He wanted new scenery, a fresh environment, a different lifestyle; his cage had been rattled.

The process of relocating to the West took him a full year. Dozens of phone calls, many interviews, and multiple flights to Denver for in-person meetings. He knew it made no sense to move to Colorado without a job, since he preferred to have some financial security while making this significant adjustment. He wasn't particular about specifically where he would resettle as long as it was close to the Rockies. Although it was a stressful year at times, the prospect of moving was also exciting. He was determined to make the move, convinced life out there would be better.

• • •

Just one year after that conversation with John, Gabe stuffed his 2006 Honda Civic with as many of his belongings as it could hold and migrated West. After moving expenses and the first and last month's rent in his new apartment, he only had a few hundred bucks left to his name. He couldn't afford any mistakes, a guiding principle he would call into use many times in the mountains.

In some ways, Gabe was right that he needed a fresh start, and it turned out to be the best decision he had made at that point in his life. But not because of being Colorado. He'd started a journey that couldn't be scripted, non-linear, and filled with more challenges (and experiences) than he could ever expect.

The beauty of the Rockies did lead to some peace in his life, and by mid-2015, he would have told anyone he'd been right about moving. He'd become a mountaineer, he had a girlfriend who he cared for, and he was about to own his first home. Yet, deep down, he knew that accomplishments and relationships can be fleeting and change in a moment.

As Gabe would learn, the briefest moments and simplest occurrences can change the course of a person's life. A thought, an idea, a vision, a random encounter. He would learn to recognize these life shifts, watershed moments that usher in new chapters, new relationships, new experiences, new perspectives. In Gabe's case this awakening of sorts was sparked by one simple question his friend asked, a question that started dramatic change.

Gabe had told himself in 2009 that, to paraphrase John Muir, the mountains were calling, and he needed to go. But in fact, it wasn't about the mountains. Mountains are beautiful, challenging, and humbling. But even so, he was deluded into believing he was being pulled toward something. What he thought was a call to new terrain was actually an escape from where he was, not geographically, but mentally, emotionally, psychologically. An escape from the lack of meaning in his life. Instead of looking inside, he was distracting himself with a new job and different venue.

It would be more than a decade later that Gabe would be able to fully understand that.

CHAPTER FIVE
ACRONYMS

Upon returning to Colorado from his week in Bolivia in mid-2015, Gabe's life carried on as it had before. He left South America in South America. The big project for him now was to complete the house he was having built and was hoping would be ready by early 2016. It was nothing elaborate, just a condo on the outskirts of Denver in a little town called Arvada, but it was exciting all the same. A bit of adulthood.

Gabe had continued his career in digital marketing and marketing strategy and had landed a good position with a renewable energy company. Finally, he was making his way and participating in the American Dream and owning his own home.

For years, Gabe felt a tinge of guilt when his family or friends invited him for dinner or a holiday celebration, knowing he couldn't reciprocate until he had a decent place of his own. He'd always lived in apartments too small to accommodate several guests. He wanted to be able to host others the way they hosted him. Now, about to have a place of his own, he envisioned having family and friends over for all kinds of events, whether it be cozy dinners or a relaxed evening with a movie, a celebratory party, or holiday festivities. Slowly but surely, he was crossing the line between his carefree twenties and true adulthood. He'd also convinced himself that having his own little corner of the world would provide peace of mind.

Until then, that had been lacking.

• • •

Reality and routine would soon remove the air from Gabe's aspirations of leading a robust and adventurous life in the mountains. He wound up doing the things he thought he was *supposed* to do, according to the dictate of society and culture. Work became his priority—pushing adventure and excitement into the backseat of his journey.

Despite the rigors of work, Gabe managed to have some fun. He told everyone back East that Colorado was a great place to live, and he meant it. The majority of people there love to do healthy things, like hike, snow ski, and camp. Growing up in the Philadelphia area, the great outdoors had much less appeal and much less opportunity.

When he first moved to Colorado, Gabe was interested in the challenging mountain skiing that Colorado had to offer, an urge stoked by his Uncle Steve who had lived in a small town called Conifer for years, just thirty miles outside of Denver. Snow skiing was great for the winter months, but what would Gabe do the rest of the year? Steve had suggested Gabe join the Colorado Mountain Club, CMC for short.

At first, he was lukewarm at best about joining CMC, but he decided to see what it was all about. He needed to build some community since he didn't know many people, and joining the group would provide a social network and a new skill set.

Gabe signed up for his first CMC course in 2011. He learned your basic hiking skills: map reading, the "10 Essentials," weather considerations, gear, etc. After that, he moved on to basic mountaineering school (BMS). There, he learned about basic rock climbing, snow travel, mountaineering team dynamics, and a bit more about advanced gear and being in alpine situations. Then, fully immersed, he took just about all of the courses that the CMC had to offer: alpine scramble, basic ice, intermediate rock, winter camping, high altitude mountaineering school, or HAMS for short. Eventually, Gabe became a HAMS instructor and even sat on CMC's board of directors. Trips with the CMC took him to places all over Colorado and to the Pacific Northwest and Mexico.

And his Uncle Steve was right: Gabe had developed a community of like-minded friends, not the least of which was his girlfriend, Anna.

• • •

Anna and Gabe had traveled all over Colorado camping and hiking. The Front Range, the San Juans, the Gores and Sangres, the Sawatch. He discovered Snowmass Lake in the Elks, which would remain one of his favorite places in the world.

By fall of 2015, he found himself content with life. He was surrounded by beauty and love. He was happy, but something deep down was missing. The peace and happiness that comes from within wasn't something he even knew how to seek.

Then, right before Thanksgiving in 2015, Anna decided to visit South America herself.

Aconcagua is a peak on the border of Argentina and Chile. At 22,837 feet, it is the highest mountain in both the Southern and Western Hemispheres. Many mountaineers' careers that start in North America eventually end up on Aconcagua as it's an excellent mountain for preparing for Denali or the higher peaks of the Himalaya. On Aconcagua, climbers get a sense of how their body and mind react to higher altitudes, and they also experience what it's like to climb in another country. Traveling to other parts of the world is always complicated and can be downright stressful; climbing expeditions are no different. Language differences, food choices, travel arrangements, medical care can at times be as difficult to overcome as scaling the mountain itself. At extreme altitudes, climbers can experience severe issues like cerebral or pulmonary edema, which unless managed quickly and appropriately, can lead to death.

Gabe's Uncle Steve had summited Aconcagua a few years earlier, and it had been on Gabe's to-do list. But Gabe was reticent, having been apprised by his uncle of how miserable life on that mountain could be.

Gabe liked climbing but didn't do well at higher altitudes. Many people who enter alpine environments experience all kinds of physical and mental challenges. Gabe reached his personal limits at around eighteen thousand feet: nausea, headaches, dizziness, and digestive issues, all conditions not conducive to summiting the world's higher peaks. Gabe was self-aware enough to know pushing himself beyond his limits would be a miserable and potentially damaging situation.

As a practical matter, Gabe couldn't travel to Aconcagua, anyway. He was short on vacation days because of his own time in South America. He was bummed he couldn't join Anna, but he was also a bit relieved. And, since the trip was in late November, he could enjoy the build up to the holidays from the comforts of home in Colorado. And it was an almost luxurious "comfort" compared to what he had seen in Bolivia.

• • •

Since Anna was going to be away for three weeks, Gabe decided to surprise her by decorating her apartment for the holidays. She would arrive home with everything ready to go. Gabe had never been much of a romantic, but he knew he could do this well.

Gabe went all out, decorating a tree—fake, but authentic-looking nonetheless—with cheery ornaments, garland, and of course multiple strands of lights to brighten the dark, winter season. He hung stockings and purchased enough battery-operated candles to brighten every window in the house. By the time he was finished, her place could rival those done up by even the most enthusiastic of Christmas decorators. He had done well.

Gabe also had time to shop for Christmas gifts in advance. Since they had a shared love for mountaineering, he knew exactly what kind of gifts to buy: magnetron and locking carabiners, new static rope, a rope bag, slings, cams, hexes, warm socks, base layers. These items may not sound sexy to the uninitiated, but he felt confident that she would love them.

The day of her return arrived, and Gabe was expecting a cheerful and grateful phone call as soon as she saw what he'd done. They'd planned to meet up the day after she landed, so he could finish his workday and she could catch up on sleep. Even though he'd tracked her and her team via GPS, he was eager to hear about her trip, just as she'd been about his trip to Bolivia. Maybe overeager.

The phone call didn't go as he'd envisioned. Some of the first words out of her mouth were, "We need to talk."

CHAPTER SIX
LIFE FALLS APART

    Returning to Anna's apartment to remove the Christmas decorations was gut-wrenching, but it had to be done. Gabe gathered up all the presents he had excitedly—and beautifully, he would add—wrapped and set out. All that planning and work to get her place looking great was effectively for nothing; he would once again face another holiday single.

    As Gabe supposed happens to most people, life blindsided him just when he was moving down that calm, comfortable path. He'd been disappointed about not spending the holidays with Anna, but he wasn't the first person in the world to be broken up with. Healing would come, and there were already signs that he and Anna would remain friends.

Nearing Christmas, he gave one of his mountaineering friends a call and shamefully explained that things hadn't worked out with Anna. Even though there was heartbreak, he knew there was a bright side; since they broke up right before Christmas, Gabe ended up with a lot of new gear.

"There's always a silver lining," his friend said. "And just like on the mountain, disappointments and setbacks, like not summiting, are necessary for real change and growth."

Gabe gritted his teeth at the pragmaticism, but knew his friend was right. Those words never seemed to help while going through a challenging time, but the more of these turning points anyone lived through, the more philosophical about them Gabe would become. He would take on opportunities to grow.

• • •

As the new year began, Gabe's cage was once again rattled. He'd only just resolved to put the discouraging end of the prior year behind, thinking that at least work was going well for him despite rumors that the company might be in financial trouble. He'd survived a round of layoffs before year's end and was feeling a bit more secure. But some mismanagement and turnover in January led to more layoffs. And his job was cut. At least he hadn't lost his position before the holiday, but this news was rough, nonetheless. First his girlfriend, now his job.

Since Gabe was now newly unemployed, he had to streamline all costs. He had just bought a new car, and now he could no longer afford the payments; he would need to unload it. Worse, he could no longer afford the new house he was having built, scheduled to be completed in the spring. The mortgage approval process had yet to be completed and he wasn't going to be approved with no money coming in. No more visions of family dinners, no more plans for having friends over for parties and events. All his daydreams of being a good host and repaying all the times people had him over? Poof, gone.

It was a surreal moment when Gabe had to walk through the

house to review for the builder the specifications in the condo plan that he'd made months before. Although now, he was no longer going to live there. It was an absurd situation, but he hoped the people who eventually bought the home would enjoy the selections he made.

Instead of fretting, Gabe immediately began applying for work. There were lots of opportunities for marketing and sales experts, especially in the booming renewable energy industry. What's more, many employers were amenable to allowing contract employees to work remotely. Gabe would vigorously beat the bushes. He was young, smart, and technically savvy. Plus, he was pursuing an advanced degree, which would surely make him even more attractive to potential employers.

Sometimes, the loss of a dream was just as painful as the loss of something Gabe was already living. These losses, now piling up, were starting to cripple him. It wasn't just things Gabe was losing; he had worked hard to build a life that now wasn't going to be his. He'd tried to put himself in a position to be the stereotypically responsible adult. That role looked so appealing; it was all *right there*.

After the walk-through, Gabe reflected back to his time in Bolivia only six months prior, and how the people and families he met didn't have much. Many had no jobs, certainly no cars, and very little in terms of what Americans consider a proper house. He'd had sympathy for them then, but now, he started to empathize. It was as if there was a new line of connection between him and the Bolivian people he'd recently met, as he was starting to walk the proverbial mile in their shoes.

But his positivity waxed and waned. The flip side was that the families in Monte Rancho had more than he did, that is if he was being honest with himself. Even though they had so few material possessions and comforts, their humble homes were filled with love and family. It was acknowledgment that poverty comes in many shapes and sizes.

Clearly it was time to regroup, Gabe had reasoned, and sometimes the universe forces a new direction. Everyone has profound experiences in their lives—a divorce, the loss of a loved one, a financial crisis. As trite as it may sound, troubles and crises appear for a reason, Gabe had concluded. *The harder you get your cage rattled, the more change you may need.*

Instead of being absorbed in despair and deep sorrow, Gabe would search for life-changing opportunities to lean into, to grow. If you can just recognize them and embrace them—even with the slightest submission—tremendous possibilities are available, he reasoned.

Leaning into change will be easier than I think. Take that baby step into your biggest fear; it can be done, he told himself.

• • •

Gabe quickly, and luckily, found a part-time job at a mountaineering shop where at least he'd be around people and not wallow all day. He figured he'd just keep busy and start to rebuild.

But it wasn't working. On one raw, rainy day in April 2016, Gabe sat in his soon-to-be-sold car outside the YMCA in Golden. It was the middle of a weekday afternoon, so the lot was mostly empty. Everything looked black and white. Having the time to go to the gym midday, rather than being at work, was a mixed blessing. He'd be pumping weights and hitting the Stairmaster, but his savings dwindled. His work experience was being wasted and the only job he had was one that doesn't pay the bills. Gabe's inner voice was loud as he looked around. Even the sidewalks were empty. The day was as bleak as his mood.

Never having been overly emotional, when a whimper rose from deep within, Gabe was caught off guard. Then, he lost all sense of time and place as he just flat out sobbed. By the time he could catch his breath, he was exhausted by the outpouring of grief, anxiety, and fear. He couldn't believe how quickly he'd gone from the highs of early December to the point at which if he didn't remind himself just to breathe from crying so hard he might pass out.

An emotional breakdown like that often provides a shift, maybe even some clarity. That's what was happening at that moment. Gabe was unknowingly moving into a new search for meaning and purpose.

But he didn't quite see it then. What he did feel, however, was that he was off course. Somewhere deep inside had sprung an awareness that real happiness and peace of mind are way better than either houses or cars, big bank accounts or a diversified stock portfolio.

For Gabe, the analogy was clear; there is the kind of rock you climb, and there is the kind of *rock* that is within every human being. The rock can be your heart, your soul, your thoughts and behaviors, your awareness. It's the true you.

For Gabe, fear had descended deep within him. *People spend billions of dollars to not take that hurtful journey,* he thought. But, he concluded, it's by taking that isolating, self-reflecting and painful path toward who you truly are when all else is stripped away that understanding can be found. *It's a connection with the truth that defines us.*

That journey is not an endless reaching for the ever higher peak, but discovering the essence you have been born to be. *What did Nietschke say?* Gabe asked himself. *"Become who you are."*

Gabe knew that an inward journey had to be taken. He had to find his core, his *rock,* to achieve peace of mind. It's then that one can start to be fearless.

Gabe knew what he needed to do, but what he really wanted at that moment was a quick fix. Finding his core would be arduous and come slowly. Again, his mind turned to Bolivia. He had felt so good helping others while there. Was that his core? Could he get out of his own head and bring that feeling back?

• • •

The job Gabe had just lost at the renewable energy company was installing large scale community solar projects—basically commercial and utility solar farms. He had often talked to a colleague there, Michelle, about the exciting work they were completing. They both enjoyed working for an environmentally conscious organization. Michelle was more on the project development side of the business, and Gabe in sales and marketing. Their conversations more or less always ended in a similar fashion: "I wish I was closer to the end user to see the positive impacts of our efforts," he had said. The work they were doing was important, but he and Michelle never saw the end results. Their discussions had gone on for months, and once she even said, "At some point, I'd like to do this type of renewable energy work in South America."

Now, on that rainy, raw, miserable day in April, in the car, it struck Gabe. He had all this spare time on his hands, and he knew people in Bolivia. Maybe he could make some connections and see if renewable energy projects *were* needed down there.

Apparently, thought Gabe, *emotional meltdowns provide space for creativity.* He wondered how many people experience major brainstorms when coming unglued mentally and emotionally. Immediately, Gabe was encouraged. Maybe the breakdown had been cathartic; maybe he was ready to start to move forward.

Gabe wasted no time. Remembering the profound lack of infrastructure in Cochabamba inspired a conversation between him and Michelle.

"What if we could somehow establish a nonprofit that could bring solar energy to underserved and underprivileged schools in Bolivia?"

"I love that idea, Michelle. And maybe the internet someday too."

"We need financial backers and a solid plan with costs breakdowns, engineering needs, permits . . ." Gabe sighed. "It's a huge undertaking, Gabe."

"Yes, but it's an inspired one. We can do this."

Enthused by the notion, they both set up a demanding schedule and made lists of people to contact. They tirelessly built the connections that helped frame and establish their new nonprofit—Pidola.

To learn more about international project development, Gabe spoke to people from not only across Bolivia, but from all over the world: England, Germany, Tanzania, Peru, Singapore, Japan, Mexico. He engaged with anyone who had experience with these sorts of projects and knowledge of doing business in South America. He was acting a little like a self-appointed economic ambassador, and the business of it all felt empowering.

All this activity brought Gabe a tremendous sense of meaning. Maybe he didn't and wouldn't soon have a significant other or children of his own, or a house, or a new car, or really anything uniquely his. *But maybe this is better,* he told himself. He believed his own inner narrative: his sense of purpose had always been a bit blurry, but the new work in South America could provide definition.

There was the new silver lining he'd needed to find, he told himself. This time it wasn't relocating to Colorado or being gifted a pile of gear at Christmas. Now that his personal and professional life had collapsed, his path was clear to do good work for the underserved people of Bolivia. *That sounds like a very rich and meaningful life.*

CHAPTER SEVEN

SI, EVO

If you search online for "Pampa Jasi," you get a neighborhood of the same name that's right outside of La Paz. That's not where Gabe was headed. On this visit to Bolivia, where he was going wasn't on any map. It was six to seven hours south-southeast of Cochabamba. Small, remote, and underserved, it was the perfect location for the new nonprofit's first project.

Michelle and Gabe had brought on another friend and colleague, Nick, to work with them on the nonprofit, and all three labored for a year to establish the foundation and operational components of the organization.

In the US, the three colleagues had completed all the necessary activities that people associate with nonprofit startups: applying for and receiving their determination letter from the IRS (now a 501(c)3), establishing a board of directors, and raising funds from donors and other corporate organizations to get operations going. They'd gone beyond the basics, too. The co-founders had met with federal-level government officials in La Paz and made connections with people at the US Department of State. They'd even somehow managed to involve the Bolivian Space Agency—the Bolivian version of NASA. They'd believed these early efforts would help them get established and ensure that their work would be well received and sustainable.

Even with all that, Bolivia was still a difficult place to start a foreign business.

In 2006, Bolivians elected a new president, Juan Evo Morales Ayma. Evo's background was different from many other Bolivian presidents in that he had been born to an Aymaran family, one of the Andean cultures that are indigenous to Bolivia, and up into Ecuador. He had great support from and connections with the local *cocoaleros*—cocoa growers in Northern and Eastern Bolivia. That meant that Evo had a strong, influential, and large constituent base. Evo was not just another politician with a Spanish background, or someone under the influence of the West, but one of the "people."

The early months and years of Evo's presidency saw Bolivia's economy grow. Thousands of citizens were able to move above the poverty line.

When Gabe was in Bolivia for his first trip with his church group, he'd seen the words *Si Evo* graffitied everywhere. Their liaisons said it loosely meant that everything was possible with Evo Morales as president. Suddenly people had jobs and access to universal healthcare and education. Young people could more easily go to college. The early socio-economic progress under his presidency led to national enthusiasm.

Evo was neither a supporter nor a fan of the US, despite American diplomatic efforts and US investment in his country. His position was that the US government had meddled in Bolivian affairs for much too long.

America's influence could be traced back to the Bolivian election in 1952, when election results were allegedly manipulated. The US had also covertly assisted various military regimes and supporting populist governments in the 1960s and '70s—the low point of American diplomatic relations. The Carter Administration had refused to recognize General Garcia Meza's government because of its ties to the drug trade, and the Reagan administration continued a similar policy. In June 1980, the US ambassador to Bolivia became a *persona non grata,* and between July 1980 and November 1981, US-Bolivian relations were suspended.

Ultimately, relationships between the US and Bolivia became so strained that most American government and business interests, including nonprofits and NGOs of all kinds, were no longer welcome. USAid had been infusing tens of millions of dollars into Bolivia to support socially beneficial projects, but even they had been pushed out. Very few US-based organizations remained during Evo Morales's presidency, and even fewer entered, if any at all. It was almost unheard of for a newly-founded US-based nonprofit to begin operations in Bolivia.

When Gabe, Michelle, and Nick were getting started, they had conversations with more than a few people who said, "You know, Bolivia is an unfriendly and socialist government. It may be hard to work there," or "There's so much opportunity (and need) for NGOs in Africa and India. Why not start there?" They'd even been told, "This is probably downright impossible."

The three didn't let the naysayers discourage them. Because they already knew people in Bolivia, specifically at the local and departmental—what Americans would call a "state"—levels, that was the easiest place to start, and then later they could work with other governments in South America. Bolivia was just their first target.

Gabe spoke with people from Food for the Hungry, the organization his church partnered with that had a footprint established in Bolivia.

Having been in Bolivia for more than thirty years doing a variety of social projects, they knew the people and the geography and had relationships with locals. An unofficial motto of the FH team was, *Where the road ends, our work begins.*

Gabe and the others were searching for locations not connected to the power grid and with no plans to connect for many years to come. Places so remote that there was no real infrastructure to speak of—no cell service, no paved roads, and in some cases, no roads at all.

• • •

Gabe had met Ali from FH on his first trip. Now she was his liaison and helped Gabe and the others by contacting authorities at different levels throughout Bolivia to locate potential project sites. Initially, two areas were in the running—one location near a town called Villa Tunari, about four hours east of Cochabamba, and the other near the town of Torotoro, about the same distance south of Cochabamba. Both communities needed the help.

The three partners decided to meet leaders in communities surrounding Torotoro in the department of Potosi. There, although paved roads were sparse, there was at least a decent network of dirt roads. Contractors would need some way to get solar panels and satellite dishes to the locations. Torotoro provided easier access than the communities near Villa Tunari.

So, Michelle, Nick, and Gabe hopped on a plane, each with a bag of clothing smaller than the luggage filled with paperwork and gifts for the local communities. Everything was starting to take shape, and solidifying Pampa Jasi as the location for the first project was the next step.

CHAPTER EIGHT
PAMPA JASI

As they began the always painful descent into La Paz, Gabe thought, *Man, how did I end up here?* As he, Michelle, and Nick made their way off the next flight, landing in Cochabamba, Gabe was groggy, of course, but excited.

Most Bolivians, especially those in the Andes, are not very tall. When Gabe walked the streets of La Paz, he was at least one head above the rest of the crowd, and two heads over some elderly women. Most Americans and Europeans stand out because of their size. But when he met their driver, Pablo, he realized he'd just met an outlier. Pablo was a massive Bolivian from outside of Santa Cruz. If there were any trouble, at six-three and at least two hundred and fifty pounds, Pablo would be a deterrent. Gabe chuckled quietly, thinking how Pablo's hands could squash his own little peanut head like a grape.

Quickly, it became apparent that Pablo's heart was proportional to his size. He was kind, generous, and accommodating, all of which was apparent even though he didn't speak much English. Pablo could always bring a smile to himself by saying *"beefe"* every time they drove past some cows. *Beefe* would forever come to mind whenever Gabe saw cattle.

The interpreter, whom the group met for the first time that day in Cochabamba, was also an outlier, a translator by trade. She had translated the Bible—not from written language to written language—into sign language. In addition to this impressive ability, she was once arrested for trying to smuggle Bibles into Iran from Turkey. The three co-founders liked her immediately.

Gabe, Michelle, Nick, Pablo, and Lidy climbed into a white Toyota 4Runner, the type of SUV necessary for the terrain ahead. As they headed out of Cochabamba, they passed the Christo de la Concordia (Cochabamba's version of Christ the Redeemer) Church in the middle of town—an impressive structure reminding them that the spiritual nature of Bolivia ran deep and that there was no lack in the cities of impressive old architecture. But after about an hour of driving through the suburbs of Cochabamba—past the previously visited Monte Rancho—Pablo turned west toward Torotoro. The towns became smaller; where there had been dozens of structures, there were now only a handful. The roads became rougher. It went from paved roads to brick roads, then gravel roads to dirt. Fewer police stations, gas stations, hospitals, and healthcare facilities. Less of everything.

The landscape around them was different, too. Cochabamba was green and somewhat tropical, whereas central Bolivia is dry and barren, even the mountains. The road was in a mile-wide valley flanked by ranges of about 2,000 feet of prominence.

The surroundings, except for the crystal-clear blue sky, felt a bit like what Gabe imagined one might experience on the planet Mars. It was beautiful. Being a mountain-loving person, Gabe enjoyed this type of landscape the most, craning his neck to look for the best routes up various ridges and peaks. And it was certainly remote.

"AAA is definitely not coming to give us a tow if we break down," Nick quipped.

Laughing about it made the anxiety of breaking down miles from anywhere on this type of terrain a tad less terrifying.

One of the more uncomfortable aspects of the drive wasn't its length, or the bumpy roads, or the constant need for bathroom breaks where there were no bathrooms. It was the dust. Driving on dirt roads leads to dirt in the vehicle. It's inevitable. By the time they reached Torotoro, everything inside the car was covered in dust, including themselves.

The small town of Torotoro was in the same valley they'd been driving through over the last few hours. A gorgeous corner of the world, it was deemed a *parque nacional* by the government. The town didn't receive too many visitors, since most of the tourists who made their way to Bolivia stayed in the north to visit the Uyuni Salt Flats, Lake Titicaca, and the Death Road. But those who made the trip south were treated to the massive Torotoro Canyon, dozens of dinosaur tracks, and centuries-old cave carvings. It looked to Gabe like a paradise for mountain bikers.

Only about a thousand people lived in Torotoro proper; it was not a large town, maybe a square mile with a central village square, which was standard for almost any South American town. A twenty-foot dinosaur statue stood proudly in the middle of the town square, and the center also had a half-dozen hotels and restaurants that catered to the few visitors.

Gabe was relieved to see that the hotel was more than adequate. A modest two-story building, the first floor housed administrative offices and then opened into a nice garden to the side—a welcome patch of green in the otherwise barren landscape. The hotel was mostly vacant, which worked out well for Gabe and his crew. They would make the dining area near the garden their remote office where they could meet.

The owner of the hotel, Lily, was kind and accommodating in typical Bolivian fashion. In her fifties, Lily was manager, cleaner, and cook, somehow juggling everything with grace and good spirits.

There was only about an hour before the group were to meet with Elio, the mayor of Torotoro. The meeting was important because Elio oversaw most of the operations not only within the town but also in the surrounding areas. Outside of Pampa Jasi's community leaders themselves, he would be the person to give final approval for the project. Everything effectively rested on his decision.

After shaking off the layer of road dust they'd accumulated, the group waited for word alerting them that Elio had returned to his office.

Gabe had presented in front of hundreds of people many times for various jobs, but this conversation was unlike any other. He was nervous and anxious. After all the planning and preparation, he felt responsible to do well. His potential new-found purpose in life hinged on this one discussion.

It's crazy how a full year of work can come down to a sixty-minute conversation, he thought.

Gabe started feeling nauseated. If Gabe failed to sell the mayor on the project his well-meaning group would be deflated and return home with nothing to show for their year's work. Gabe had even more at risk. He confided in Michelle that he felt like his entire life had led up to this moment. Michelle's eyes widened, telling him to breathe. Perhaps he'd shared too much.

"Sorry Michelle. But I have invested so much of myself into this project. It's an opportunity for me to restart my life, to dedicate myself to something important, to give myself a sense a purpose."

"I do understand, Gabe. We put a lot of effort into this and I'm confident things will work out for us. This is a great opportunity for this community, and I am betting the mayor knows that as well."

After that awkward moment, Gabe walked separately from the group to calm himself. He focused on his breathing and tried to relax and clear his mind. Everything seemed to be moving in slow motion. It felt like he was walking through honey.

As they entered the offices, people were scurrying around attending to daily tasks. The curious looks that everyone gave the Americans as they walked by suggested they probably didn't get many foreign visitors into the building. Gabe imagined the workers thinking to themselves, *What the hell do these idiots want?*

Elio's office was up a few flights of stairs. It wasn't large or impressive as are so many mayoral offices in US cities. In fact, it was a tight fit for all the people now crammed into it. Introductions took a while. In addition to the mayor, some of his advisers and members of the town council, plus one of the community leaders from Pampa Jasi, were also present. Greetings were the Bolivian standard: a handshake, a half hug of the sort you would give your aunt, with plenty of distance involved, and a second handshake. Given how nervous and anxious Gabe was, he botched every greeting, stumbling through words and only awkwardly connecting with these strangers. *Not a great start, he thought. Confidence . . . be confident,* he told himself.

With only one window, and the sun on the other side of the building, the room was dark. The mayor of Torotoro wasn't like Pablo. He was a typically sized Bolivian standing just a couple inches over five feet. What he lacked in height, however, he made up for in presence. His kindness showed in his eyes. He seemed like the people Gabe had met on prior trips, local officials who cared about every one of their constituents.

After the *mucho gustos,* Lidy, Michelle, Nick, and Gabe got into the rhythm and flow of the presentation. The energy in the room was positive and welcoming, and Gabe felt much more at ease, especially since he could see everyone's facial expressions. Their initial reactions were even energized. He described Pidola's intentions, the benefits to the community, and the short history and mission of the nonprofit organization. Questions from members of the mayor's entourage ensued:

"Why our village?"

"How much will this cost us?"

"Who are you again?"

After an hour of back-and-forth, Elio and his advisers welcomed them to the community. Unofficially, the project was approved.

An enormous weight had been lifted off Gabe's shoulders. All the prep, all the planning, all the effort for that sixty-minute conversation. It had paid off. He almost broke down in happy tears overcome by joy. They had cleared the first hurdle—quite possibly the tallest one. The people of Pampa Jasi would definitely embrace the project.

Gabe and his contingent left the mayor's office and went back to the hotel to get dinner, but they didn't have much time to relax and enjoy the moment. The visit to Pampa Jasi was early the next morning.

• • •

The next day started off with a bang—literally. In smaller towns and villages all throughout Bolivia, gunfire welcomes the days when celebrations are taking place. This celebration had nothing to do with visiting Americans; it was to recognize the opening of a new road in the area. Awakening to gunshots versus an alarm clock startled Gabe. It was a sign that the day would be another educational one for three colleagues from Colorado.

Gabe was less nervous about that day's conversations, but still focused on what he needed to accomplish as the words *"be confident"* resonated within. They had managed to do well with the mayor, and now they were to meet the people who would be directly benefiting from the project. It was thrilling, exactly the scenario Michelle, Nick and he had discussed the year before when they got started.

First, though, they had a three-hour drive from Torotoro to Pampa Jasi.

Torotoro was remote, but not overly difficult to reach for anyone who really wanted to see the area's attractions. Pampa Jasi was an entirely different scenario. The stone roads of Torotoro led to dirt roads, and almost immediately started to climb one of the ridges directly outside of town. Winding up over the switchbacks, they eventually came to a ridge that Pablo would drive on for the next two-and-a-half hours. The road was wide enough for one vehicle, but two? That presented a constant challenge. Every time they passed a vehicle heading in the opposite direction, they held their collective breaths, since one slip would send them fifteen hundred feet down the side of the mountain. Despite the precarious and nerve-racking ride, the drive was undeniably beautiful. The occasional sighting of an Andean condor, Bolivia's national bird, was a welcomed surprise.

It was the dry season, and just as when they traveled into Torotoro the day before, the skies were bluebird. From the road, Gabe could see a hundred miles in all directions. Locals were walking down the road, as most Bolivian villagers didn't have cars. Each passerby would ask for a ride, many times in Quechua, the local native language, and Pablo subsequently gave permission. *Sí, claro!*

Even though the 4Runner was filled with gear and its four passengers, the group was always as accommodating as possible. One of the benefits of Bolivians being a bit smaller was that they could fit into a crammed vehicle more easily.

Some villages were a full day's roundtrip walk from Torotoro, and in many cases people walked all that way just to make a phone call or speak to a local official. At one point, Gabe turned to Nick and said in a low voice, "Anyone having a serious medical emergency in this area would be in trouble." Another benefit of their projects.

• • •

Eventually the road wound down off the ridge and into a valley to the west, mountain walls on both sides. The buildings of Pampa Jasi were becoming visible in the distance. There was a total of six: a schoolhouse, a storage building, and four buildings which some of the town residents called home. The schoolhouse was built soundly out of concrete and was relatively new, but the other buildings were mainly mud-brick and straw gathered from the area. They were roughly the size of a couple of American backyard sheds joined together. Together, the building formed a circle around the center—a village center square of dirt.

Adjacent to the main buildings of the village was the all-important soccer field. Since the area could probably be defined as a desert, the field was just dirt, but it did have two metal goals. No nets. To the rear of the soccer field was the "bathroom," another example of the lack of proper facilities in Pampa Jasi. No running water, no toilets, no outhouses. Just an open latrine on the far side of the soccer field. Toilet paper and trash scattered around.

The 4Runner attracted attention. Since a semblance of a dirt road skirted the town, vehicles weren't uncommon. What was unusual was three foreigners stepping out of a stopped vehicle: Gabe with blue eyes and a beard; Michelle with blond hair; Nick who stood well over six feet.

Most of the adults in Torotoro had seen foreigners, but many of the smaller and younger children hadn't. Just like in Monte Rancho, a shy, uncertain curiosity arose from the children. As they walked through the village introducing themselves to the community leaders, the Americans waved and said, "*Que tal. ¿Cómo estás?*" to the children and try to get a handshake from them. The thing that worked best to start and build a relationship was a simple friendly smile.

Once the initial hesitancy had passed, the children warmed to their new group of visitors, especially after receiving the gifted soccer balls. Gabe knew the standard practice of giving gifts, and they instantly became much more welcome. A quick game of soccer ensued. A strong sense of nostalgia overwhelmed Gabe as the group started to kick the soccer balls around. It had probably been thirty years since Gabe had played the game as a kid growing up just north of Philadelphia. *Life is not linear,* Gabe thought. And this was the classic case.

Gabe would never have anticipated that "sports" diplomacy might change the world of these children and their town. *Perhaps,* he thought, *it should be employed more often.*

Gabe had forgotten how bad he was at the beautiful game, so he was almost relieved when the fun and games ended and meetings between the various members of the community and Gabe's group began. Most of the community representatives were teachers, since many of the received benefits of the project would be educational. One by one, more adults from the surrounding homes came to say hello and participate in a planned town meeting.

Teachers set up a table in front of the schoolhouse, and for an hour teachers and villagers alike asked about the project and goals as well as reasons for choosing their village. Questions were just like the ones from the day before in Torotoro:

"Who are you?"

"What are you doing here?"

"Why our village?"

"How much will this cost us?"

It was the ideal conversation. The community's embrace was vital. It wouldn't work to impose an outside group's vision on the residents. That couldn't be sustained. Acceptance, sufficient planning, and enthusiasm within the community was critical for reaping long-term benefits.

After an hour of productive and increasingly warmer conversation, community members expressed their approval of the project.

Gabe's tension had now finally abated. They'd found the location for their pilot project. A schoolhouse serving just shy of one hundred children in remote Pampa Jasi would now have access to renewable energy and internet.

• • •

The community leaders wanted their North American visitors to meet some of the families living outside of the main cluster of buildings as well. In the Torotoro area, potable water was a scarce resource, so locals had questions about how to best get water drawn from a well or a nearby creek. None of the three from Pidola was knowledgeable about water systems, but they engaged in conversations to learn about other needs. There was always the possibility that they could find an expert back in the States who could help.

The city of Potosi was just about one hundred miles south of Pampa Jasi, and the group headed in that direction. Along the way, they picked up a goat and stopped at the roadside to talk with a family who had questions about accessing water from a small creek nearby. They walked a few hundred yards into the middle of a small plateau, still in the valley where Pampa Jasi was located. There, they came across the home of a family of four: each of their two rooms was at most ten-by-ten feet.

There was no electricity or running water. Their water was stored in old gasoline containers. They had poorly constructed mud walls and just a tin roof loosely attached on top.

It took Gabe a few moments to digest what he was seeing, and then that now familiar heartbreak hit him. How, for the rest of his life, could he ever validate complaining about anything? The shame of having whined about anything, ever, washed over him again, as it had on his first trip to Bolivia. It was more than humbling, and their visit with that family was the kind of thing he'd never forget.

• • •

Back in Pampa Jasi after dinner, most of the adults were sitting around a fire in the area encircled by community buildings. It was a cool, clear, dry night, and everyone was in good spirits. Some were singing, and one man was playing a guitar in Latin fashion; others were engaged in cheery conversation. Laughter rang out now and then. Gabe sat off to the side, alone in his thoughts, reflecting on the events of the past thirty-six hours. He had a nagging feeling that while the trip was hugely successful, it wasn't enough. There was so much more to be accomplished, so much more required, even just in this one little village. Especially after visiting the family on the plateau with *absolutely* nothing. He felt good about the success of the day, and fortunate that he now had the opportunity to make a difference in these people's lives. He knew that wasn't something many relate to. But it still wasn't enough. Another familiar feeling was there. *More is needed.*

Gabe did, however, have a bit of peace of mind and comfort that he hadn't felt in some time, maybe even ever. Staring into the fire, zoned out, he felt ever surer that he'd finally found his life's calling. Quietly, he was brimming with hope. Not only for Pampa Jasi, but for himself.

Gabe thought helping as many people as he possibly could was the answer to his inner driving question.

CHAPTER NINE
LA LUZ!

About six months after that first visit to Pampa Jasi—and just short of Thanksgiving 2017—Michelle and Gabe were back in Torotoro preparing to launch the pilot project in Pampa Jasi. This trip had a new set of hurdles. In order to plan and manage both the solar panel and satellite internet installations, Gabe and Michelle arrived before the installers, who would be visiting the village of Pampa Jasi the following day. Managing people whose language you don't speak was no easy task. Also, there were no connected communication devices, and no way to show the workers where they were headed.

Gabe thought back to Nick's comment from the last visit about

AAA and said, "Google Maps has some work to do." Pampa Jasi wasn't even on any *printed* maps. Coordinating teams from all over the country to meet at a specific place and time was a challenge.

Plus, punctuality was not a Bolivian priority as Gabe would learn after a conversation with an official at the Ministry of Education in La Paz. They needed more time to review the various topics they were speaking about, so Gabe decided to schedule an additional meeting the following week. He asked in his broken Spanish, "What day and time should I come by?" The government official answered that the following Tuesday was his most available day. That was great, but Gabe wanted to get a specific time on Tuesday.

"Tuesday," the official repeated.

"Morning or afternoon?" Gabe asked, getting frustrated, and hopeful to get at least some idea.

"Tuesday." It was the official's final response.

When Gabe returned on that Tuesday morning, the official wasn't even in the office, or even the city.

"The people are wonderful here," Gabe would say to Michelle. "But there is no sense of urgency. Everything moves at its own pace. Keeping this project on schedule is going to be a problem."

"Relax, Gabe," Michelle replied with a chuckle. "You're still on American time. The clock moves slower in Latin America."

• • •

Lily, the owner and operator of the hotel where Michelle and Gabe had once again booked rooms, graciously offered to cook a big dinner as she figured they'd be missing friends and family during the Thanksgiving holiday.

"We are honored, Lily," Gabe said, with Michelle nodding her agreement. "You don't have to cook us anything. Never mind something special." Nonetheless, they were flattered and honored.

Five of them—Lily, Gabe, Michelle, Lidy, and Pablo—all huddled in the small kitchen helping to prepare the meal. Lily, a huge Michael

Bolton fan, had one of his albums playing in the background. She always did, and she was usually singing along, whether she knew the meaning of the words or not. It was also unclear what Pablo thought about Lily's musical preferences.

Because Gabe's cooking skills were at the time very basic, he was assigned duties that suited his talents: setting the table and cleaning the dishes at various intervals in the preparation. The others were busy making gravy, potatoes, bread, and a variety of standard Bolivian side dishes.

"We don't have turkey, I'm afraid, so I'll be cooking a chicken," Lily had announced earlier. However, there was no chicken in the fridge. Gabe had his suspicions, and when he heard a ruckus in the garden, he knew he'd been right. In a couple of hours, the group sat down to a lovely meal of freshly killed poultry glazed with honey mustard and stuffed with rice.

Gabe raised his glass. "To Lily, for helping to make this Thanksgiving more memorable than most!"

"Salud!" Michelle added.

• • •

The morning that Pidola's first project would be launched, Pablo, Michelle, Lily, and Gabe rose early to make the three-hour trek to Pampa Jasi, meanwhile finalizing preparations for all the other activities. They had brought with them several laptops and computers donated by individuals and organizations in the US. Solar power and the internet would be great, but they wouldn't be very meaningful without the appropriate hardware.

At the village, community leaders again welcomed Michelle and Gabe, and all went to work setting up the computers in the schoolhouse. Everything was in order after about an hour; all that was missing was power and signal.

Miraculously, the solar panel and satellite internet installers arrived on time and got to work. Their tasks were critical to the day's success—installing eight solar panels and one satellite dish behind the schoolhouse and securing all this equipment with some simple fencing. In just a handful of hours, the power went on. The small group walked into the schoolhouse and flipped the light switch to ensure that the connection worked.

"¡La luz! ¡La luz!" shouted a small girl, about five years old.

It worked.

An hour later, the satellite internet was successfully connected to both the computers and wireless modem in the room that was now the school's new computer area. But then, all the computer screen activity froze when nearly every adult tried to connect their phone to the wireless network. With so many devices all connecting at once, downloading who knows what, it took a bit of time. Eventually the rush to upload abated and shouts of satisfaction were heard.

All eighty-eight children attending the school and their teachers and community members now had power and the internet. Pidola had connected them to the rest of the world.

But the day wasn't over. The final task was configuring all the computers and laptops, one by one. The team got busy, but there was much to do, and daylight would soon be fading. That meant the group risked making the trek home over the narrow, meandering mountain road in the dark.

"No way," Gabe said to Michelle and the others. "We barely made it here alive in daylight."

Michelle laughed. "I thought you were a brave mountaineer. Since when are rock climbers scared of heights?"

"Sounds like he's more scared of the dark," Pablo teased.

"Climbing mountains with ropes and anchors is one thing," Gabe said. "Going over a cliff in an SUV is quite another."

All agreed. They had taken the community as far as they could and then left the remaining tasks for the teachers to finish.

Back at the hotel, the team celebrated with Lily and some of the other visitors. But Gabe felt less than fulfilled, just like when he'd visited Bolivia for the first time and he and his church group did less than he had hoped they would. Always, for Gabe, came the feeling of *not enough*. No peace of mind. He was disappointed that the setting sun had forced the team to leave a bit of work undone.

It would have been great to have completed everything that day. But it wasn't just that; Gabe wanted to do more. More not only in Pampa Jasi, but for all the other Pampa Jasis in South America.

More to be done.

CHAPTER TEN

MOVING DOWN SOUTH

While Michelle, Nick, and Gabe had been working on the pilot project, there had been a conversation that stemmed from a comment Gabe had made to the others months before the launch. A seemingly harmless, half-hearted comment: "If Pidola gets off the ground and we have a chance to do some additional work, I'll move to Bolivia to get our operations set up."

Gabe hadn't been doing much of anything else of significance at the time. But the closer they got to launching the pilot project—as well as establishing the nonprofit as an actual legal entity—those words started to come to life. *Do what you say you're going to do,* he had admonished himself.

Some months before his departure to Bolivia, Gabe had found and accepted a position working remotely for a website development company. It was a job he could do from anywhere with sufficient connectivity and phone service. The role aligned perfectly with a potential move to South America. It gave Gabe and the others the flexibility they needed to move their efforts forward.

Gabe reasoned that he had lived overseas before, so it wouldn't be a massive leap into the unknown to spend a year in Bolivia. Here was this great opportunity to make a significant impact on thousands of lives. It was almost a no-brainer decision. Sure, he'd be far away from all his family and friends, living in a country where he didn't really know anyone, never mind the language or the details of day-to-day living. Yet, the pull to do something altruistic, something significant to make this world a better place, overpowered his reluctance.

Can I afford it?
Is it crazy, stupid?
What will I be sacrificing?
How can I not do this?

His mental wheel was turning; thoughts circled. And then they circled faster.

Gabe had read and heard stories about people at the end of their days almost never stating that they wished they'd *not* done that one adventurous thing when they had the opportunity. Indeed, when asked what their biggest regrets are, most say that they wish they'd taken more advantage of opportunities and regretted never pushing thresholds or testing their limits. Of course, in many cases, people can't be cavalier with their lives due to family responsibilities, financial limitations, or countless other reasons. Gabe, however, was unencumbered. His dance card was empty.

This is the perfect time in my life, and the perfect opportunity, for this kind of endeavor, he thought.

The owners of the company Gabe worked for were fully supportive of his South American adventure. They were happy to let him go part-time so that the rest of his workday could be for Pidola's operations . . . and Spanish classes. Having Gabe in that part of the world might even create an opportunity for the company, so the arrangement could be a win-win.

Going part-time would cut his salary in half, but Gabe figured he'd still be making a wage in a country where the cost of living was substantially less expensive than in the US.

Could Gabe afford to do such a thing while maintaining the condo he'd recently bought in Colorado? The remote marketing job he had landed enabled him to complete the purchase from a few years earlier. But his monthly mortgage payment was steep. *No problem,* he told himself. *I'll rent it out. It'll all work fine.*

• • •

Michelle, Nick, and Gabe agreed that he'd give it one year to see how far they could push forward their work in Bolivia. So, the planning started, and an avalanche of questioning and self-doubt and questions ensued:

Where should I live?
How do I keep myself safe?
How quickly can I learn a new language?
How long does the travel visa last?
How will I get around in this unknown country?
What happens if I get sick?
How much will my visa cost me this time?
Am I doing the right thing?
What the hell am I doing?

It's one thing to move from one city to another in the United States and know how most things work and what was needed, like getting a new driver's license, transferring internet, updating your addresses. It's quite another thing to move to a foreign country where everything can, and will, be entirely different. Just planning and getting prepared for the plane ride and entering the country would be exhausting. Among the most stressful tasks would be background checks at the state, federal, and international level. Over the course of just a couple months, he was fingerprinted more than he ever anticipated that he'd be in his entire life. To obtain a Bolivian work visa, he needed all these background checks to ensure they weren't letting a criminal into the country to live. He had to confirm that he had a clean record with the Colorado Bureau of Investigations, the FBI, and Interpol. It's like getting a comprehensive health check, and he was relieved to learn he had a clean bill of criminal health.

Next was finding a place to live in Bolivia. If he were moving to Denver, it would be easier to figure out the best neighborhoods with good local supermarkets, a decent gym, and a few good coffee shops. But he knew next to nothing about living in Latin America.

Should I live closer to where the projects would potentially be?

Should I live closer to where large businesses were clustered to help find corporate sponsors?

What about being near federal government offices?

How will I find an apartment?

How does an apartment lease work for a foreign national?

Does Bolivian law even have apartment leases?

Gabe was lucky. One of Pidola's primary points of contact, who would later become Pidola's accountant in Bolivia, had a place for him to stay. Luis's mother-in-law rented out a small apartment in La Paz, in the expat-friendly neighborhood of Sopocachi. Gabe had never been there and hadn't even seen pictures. But his gut instinct or sixth sense or whatever you want to call it told him that the location would be perfect. Knowing the owners would give him more peace of mind. Overthinking was not necessary with this requirement.

Eventually things started to come together. Background checks were nearly complete, and he had taken the apartment. Gabe was close to ready—at least physically. As part of the final preparations, Michelle, Nick, the Pidola board, and Gabe held a small fundraising event for their upcoming and to-be-determined projects. They'd had the foresight to bring some things back from Bolivia for a silent auction: alpaca sweaters and hats, gloves, jewelry, trinkets, and more. After donations at the auction, they felt like professional fundraisers. It was a success.

The event doubled as a bit of a going-away party for Gabe, as well. He was moving the following week. If there was ever a situation that made him feel like he was attending his own funeral, this was it. Colorado friends all came to wish him good luck. He wondered if there were others who probably came to say good riddance. But whatever. He was off to South America. To do good things.

It was a special night. Gabe seldom found himself surrounded by so many people who truly cared about him. Such occasions are rare: a family wedding, a milestone birthday, maybe another situation or two. It was all bittersweet; he was enthusiastic about this new chapter, but also melancholic about leaving friends and Colorado life behind.

• • •

Just one week later, Gabe stepped onto the plane with a mixed bag of emotions: excitement, anxiety, optimism, trepidation. Colorado was where, for the first time in his life, he'd felt that he was in the place that he was supposed to be. For nearly ten years, he'd lived out West and had so many amazing experiences. He was close to his extended family, had built a community of friends and fellow mountain climbers, and had even finished grad school. Now, he was leaving that life behind.

But beneath all those emotions, there was, once again, a feeling that something significant in his life was missing, something deeply personal. It was, Gabe concluded, not having a family of his own yet; he didn't even have a significant other, so the prospect of marriage seemed far off, making Gabe feel lonely and isolated.

In American culture, success often is measured by career, spouse, kids, home, big bank account. Life's bingo card. Gabe couldn't help but shrink next to that measuring stick.

Ah, in your thirties and you don't have a wife and kids.

Nice little condo, but not a real house for a family.
Making enough money to get by, but no real savings.
A remote job, but no real career path.

All too often, he'd allowed these thoughts to make him feel like a failure. Perhaps he would find contentment in South America. Gabe was entering an almost completely unknown world, physically and metaphysically.

CHAPTER ELEVEN
WHY BOLIVIA?

Another descent into La Paz began, this time with the guy in the seat next to Gabe stirring, then leaning back into the window with a blanket over his face, and snoring, again.

Gabe grimaced. How was it possible this guy had slept his way through this entire flight? He'd even slept through meal service, ignoring the lights, flight attendant interruptions, everything.

Gabe himself had been awake the whole way, although he hadn't eaten much, either. Anxiety about the safety of the plane, and what he would face once in Bolivia, had his mind and stomach churning.

As on his prior trips to Bolivia, the closer the miniature airplane on the TV screen in front of him got to La Paz, the more he wondered, *How the hell did I get here?* That familiar inner question was followed by a mixed bag of emotions, including excitement and anxiousness—enough tension to add to the altitude headache he now grudgingly accepted would soon hit him like a sledgehammer.

Generally, these days, Gabe did his best to be grateful. No matter how shitty life felt on any particular day, he knew he had little to complain about. On this trip, he was particularly aware that he was lucky to be heading to South America once again, this time on a project of his own creation. Most of his friends and acquaintances in Colorado couldn't place Bolivia on a map. One person at the going away party friends and colleagues had given him had actually said, "Bolivia… that's in Eastern Europe, right?" Confusing Bolivia with Bulgaria.

As the guy in the next seat stretched under his blanket, Gabe once again broke into the cold sweat that accompanied him at the end of every flight he'd taken into La Paz.

The flight attendants coursed down the aisle collecting trash and gesturing to passengers to put their seat backs upright, and when the passenger next to him didn't budge, Gabe gently nudged him with his elbow to put his seat up. The guy groaned but emerged from his blanket and yawned.

"Thanks, man," he said, righting himself and passed some trash to the attendant. "What's bringing you to La Paz?"

Just then, the plane bounced a bit, and the seat belt sign flashed. Gabe's stomach lurched. Maybe talking about his project—what's bringing him to La Paz—would distract him a bit from his immediate concerns.

"Trying to get a nonprofit off the ground," Gabe began.

Gabe told the same story that still didn't feel stale. So many people had asked him, "Why Bolivia?" He explained his first visit with the church group that participated in efforts like building an irrigation system, assisting with the construction of a church or public project, helping family farmers, or some combination of all three. He added that the people of Bolivia had a lot to teach the world, including how to live with more peace but without as much material wealth or as many creature comforts. And he gave him the super quick elevator pitch about Pidola.

"I also climb. This trip, I'm hoping to have time and money to do a high peak."

"I've done some climbing," the guy said.

As the typical end-of-flight preparations happened around them, Gabe and his seatmate talked mountains. Gabe barely noticed the time pass. But there was no escaping the landing distress. He mopped the sweat off his forehead with his sleeve to prevent it from dripping into his eyes. He leaned back, breathed deeply, and tried to relax. Instead, his mind filled with the physical challenges he'd confronted that first trip. The plane was in major descent mode at this point, and it was not the smoothest ride. The plane ride seemed to mimic his life.

The sound of the landing gear descending brought the two of them to attention. Gabe was resigned to a gauntlet he'd run before. Gabe grimly steeled himself to deplane and face the altitude change, the cold, and customs.

Little did Gabe know, but those brief conversations in English would now be very few and far between.

CHAPTER TWELVE
NEVER COMFORTABLE IN BOLIVIA

Gabe landed in what was now a slightly more familiar city. He was expecting many of the same challenges, even though he knew there would be new ones, too. He thought of the Greek philosopher Heraclitus who wrote, *"No man ever steps in the same river twice, for it's not the same river and he's not the same man."* The lesson: change and transformation are part of what a human should embrace more often. Without growth, even the tiniest of steps, that water becomes stagnant, tepid... maybe even boring.

This trip was to be something completely new in many ways, and Gabe was thrilled about the opportunity to achieve his lofty goals of establishing and funding hundreds more projects like Pampa Jasi. This time he wasn't part of a group who would help just a few Bolivian families. He was going to make a permanent positive difference for thousands. However, it appeared he was going to start this ambitious trip inauspiciously. He realized soon after disembarking that the only pair of pants he had was the pair he had on.

Gabe always attempted to be a careful planner. In Colorado, he'd thought of everything. The required documents, the drop-off and pickups from the airports, an apartment, plans for his initial days in-country and meetings with people all over La Paz. He'd carefully and systematically packed his bags, all six of them. The minor detail he'd missed. The Bolivian transportation authority, the ATT, allows travelers to enter with only five bags. That he'd quickly learn at the check-in counter in Denver.

Gabe was decent at thinking on his feet. There had to be a shipping carrier at Denver International, right?

Nope, no longer in service.

No problem. He called his aunt, who had driven him to the airport, and she rushed back. She'd ship it to him. He gave her the smallest one—the less weight, the lower the shipping costs. Three of the bags had heavy mountaineering gear. Unfortunately, in the stress and hurry of the moment, Gabe hadn't stopped to consider what was in that light bag; he'd be wearing the same pair for the next six weeks since shipping to Bolivia is glacially slow.

• • •

Bolivian Customs wasn't bad. The visa cost increased only slightly this time. But Gabe was exhausted not only from the travel but also from the mix of emotions. There was also that untimely, negative inner voice. *What if I fail?* Failure hadn't really occurred to Gabe before leaving. It wasn't on the initial list of questions he'd been asking himself. Focusing on the variety of steps to enter a foreign country didn't allow extra space for fear. Meeting each small goal provided perhaps a false sense of security about the more important, long-term goals.

A seasoned hiker and mountain climber didn't work without a good map, a compass, and the right basic equipment. So Gabe crafted a detailed plan. It was all laid out. But still, it was uncharted territory, and in uncharted territory, even the best of plans could fall short. Sometimes the mountain just doesn't want you to summit.

But for now, everything was okay, because there, waving across a crowd of Bolivians picking up passengers, was the person who had offered to collect him—Luis, the accountant Gabe and his partners at Pidola had hired. Gabe had met him on his first trip to Bolivia; he worked with several other nonprofits, including the one through which Gabe had volunteered. And although they'd only met a couple of times, Luis's easy and engaging smile was shining from across the expanse of people juggling for position by baggage pickup. Gabe didn't know him too well, but he was recommended by various acquaintances and was friendly and open. Which wasn't unusual for Bolivians, in Gabe's experience, but this guy took it to a whole new level. He'd even helped Gabe by finding him the apartment via Luis's mother-in-law, which had a building with an open flat.

"How was the flight?" Luis asked, grabbing one of the three bags Gabe had already retrieved and piled together. Luis's English was practically perfect, which had been another selling point in hiring him.

When Gabe turned to answer, Luis was already halfway to the exit.

"I've got one more piece of luggage," Gabe called out, pointing to the carousel.

Luis looked over his shoulder and stopped. "More? You're kidding, right?"

Sheepishly, Gabe nodded and was momentarily grateful that the sixth piece was still in the United States.

"I hope we can get it all in my vehicle," Luis said, frowning. It wasn't clear if Luis's comment included disgusted at how much gear Gabe had brought or ashamed of the size of the car he was driving. He plodded back and took hold of the handle of another large suitcase.

Gabe hoped his stuff would all fit, too, and was immediately aware of how he looked to his new colleague. He had more gear than the family of four that was pushing their luggage rack through the revolving airport doors. He knew how few of the essentials Bolivians had. What he thought he would need in a year must have looked absurd to others. In fact, strangers stared at him, mouths almost open, as they dragged the luggage toward the exit.

Outside, Gabe recognized that it was going to be tricky getting it all loaded, but somehow, between the two of them, they crammed it all in, partly by pulling the front seats up as far as they could possibly go. Not a huge problem for Luis, but he was taller than the typically short, stout Boliviano. Both his and Gabe's knees were at their chins. Uncomfortable. The beat-up Suzuki that looked like it was manufactured twenty years ago was about to be transformed into a clown car.

Niceties about the flight concluded, Luis explained they'd head to his home first for a meal. With Bolivians, there was always a welcome meal. Gabe would have preferred going directly to his apartment, as he was exhausted and didn't feel like holding conversations, but he also knew from experience that you shouldn't reject Bolivian hospitality and a home-cooked meal. If he wanted this relationship to get off on the right foot, he was going to meet Luis's wife and two children. This morning. *Oh no. Would the rest of the family speak English? Likely not.* Inwardly, he groaned.

• • •

There is always something exciting about a city waking itself up for the business of the day. La Paz was like any major city in the world, alive and full of traffic at almost any hour. At least as it was so early in the day, and they wouldn't have to fight the worst of Bolivian rush-hour traffic. Gabe tried to take in all of the passing activities on the streets in order to stay awake.

Beneath the dominating Cordillera Real range, La Paz opened up like a bowl with the Choqueyapu River, often just called the La Paz River, flowing through it north to south. Unlike other cities worldwide, the wealthier neighborhoods were downstream in La Paz, as they were built when the city was first settled, and it was practical to be near a stable source of water. The city then expanded upward toward the mountains, which continued through the ensuing decades. It was a compact metropolis in which nature and urbanity, ancient churches and drab socialist architecture collide, the classic potpourri of sights and sounds. Plus, the gigantic aerial spider web of the city's gondola system, the *Teleferico,* contributed a sort of otherworldly science fiction vibe.

Suddenly, Gabe squinted and craned his neck so fast he practically gave himself whiplash. Had he just seen a bunch of people dressed like zebras crossing the road? They disappeared around the corner. His eyes were wide as he turned toward Luis and realized he'd missed something important in his dramatic family narrative. Luis was clearly waiting for him to contribute with a comment, maybe even some sympathy.

"Sorry," Gabe said, admitting he'd lost the thread. "I'm pretty out of it from the jet lag." The last thing he was going to share was that he might be hallucinating. Maybe none of it was happening. The scenery, the storytelling . . . *zebras?*

• • •

Gabe was by now well aware that morning, noon, or night, a Bolivian family sharing their home with a guest offers some combination of chicken, quinoa, potatoes, and corn. Two adorable kids were chatty and playing nearby. Neither they nor their mother spoke English even in the slightest, but they were exceedingly friendly, and Gabe found their home welcoming. It was modest but tidy, like so many of the residences in Luis's neighborhood.

The concrete structure and lack of light made the family's apartment far from cozy, despite the typical South American décor of bright colors, fascinating objects, and pillows and blankets everywhere. After their meal, the adults took the stairs to the roof to enjoy the incredible view, a benefit of where they lived that compensated for the modest structures.

"Is that Huayna Potosi?" Gabe asked.

Luis had a lot of facts to share. At about six thousand meters in altitude, Huayna Potosi within the northern mountain range in El Alto was the most popular climb for tourists, making it at times almost as busy as a New York City sidewalk. At least compared to other, more challenging peaks in the neighborhood. Gabe knew his mountains, but at this point, he was not only jetlagged but also practically comatose from the meal. He let Luis talk, and Luis seemed to enjoy being listened to. By now, Gabe didn't even have to nod or comment.

Gabe thought again about the pull to the mountains. He would never forget the stark and stunning beauty of the winter in the Andes, especially in the Altiplano, or high plains of Bolivia. When he'd first seen them, he'd fallen in love, part of why he was here now. For days on end, the sky is crystal clear, the perfect backdrop for the snow- and glacier-covered peaks that almost completely surround La Paz.

His thoughts drifted. He was grateful he'd been so well fed. That way, he wouldn't have to negotiate a grocery store on his first day. Just the idea of it gave him indigestion. *Will they accept my credit card? How will I know how much to pay?* Like the actual cost of items, not what they were charging the naive tourist who could barely count out the right change. He'd have to face reality soon enough. Still, so many unknowns.

• • •

It was afternoon by the time they headed to Gabe's new apartment in Sopocachi, just adjacent to downtown La Paz. Luis navigated his ancient, sputtering Suzuki through the maze of government and commercial buildings and into Gabe's new neighborhood. He'd picked the area for two reasons: it was close to the offices he'd have to frequent to meet people who would support Pidola's work, and it was La Paz's trendier neighborhood, flush with restaurants, coffee shops, and stores.

Once again, Gabe was oblivious to Luis's chatter. He ticked off boxes within the neighborhood while they were driving. A supermarket only about eight blocks from his building. *Check.* The Teleferico station, five blocks from his new home. *Got it.* A gym, laundromat, barber, hardware store, dry cleaner. *Excellent.* More than one park. *Awesome.* A couple of decent looking restaurants. *Even better.* Things were looking up. This neighborhood and its amenities would be a blessing. *And look, a police station.* Safety right around the corner from his place.

As they rolled up to the building, Gabe's lack of extra pairs of pants came roaring back into his consciousness. It would feel so good to get a shower and into clean clothing.

"I should know this," he said haltingly, a little embarrassed. "But what's my address again? I have a box coming to me from home and need to get the details to my aunt."

Luis turned. His expression was strange, a little tentative. "No one told you?"

Gabe took a breath. That sounded ominous. "Told me what?"

"You can't get things shipped here directly to your home address. There's no postal service."

"No postal service in La Paz?" Gabe asked. "Is there a strike or something?" Strikes were very common among Bolivia's laborers.

Luis chuckled and shook his head. "Clearly no one filled you in, Gabe. The postal service in Bolivia was shut down years ago."

Gabe stared at his new friend and colleague. "You're kidding."

Luis just shrugged and swerved into a space. "You'll have to pick up packages from DHL." He took his key out of the ignition.

"That sounds expensive," Gabe said. *First zebras, and now no postal service. Here we go.*

"A client of mine shipped one document to me recently from the

States, just one single page," Luis said. He opened his door and put one leather-clad foot out onto the street. "She said it cost ninety-nine US dollars." *Getting my pants was going to cost a fortune.*

• • •

The apartment was on the corner of Sotomayor and Munos Cornejo, between Zamudio Plaza and Zebra Park. *More zebras.* It was an unassuming building, made of what looked like red clay. On the first floor was a married couple with two kids. Gabe figured he could work on his Spanish by talking with the children, an unexpected blessing. The rest of the building was also a family affair in that on the second floor was an elderly woman who seemed to be about two hundred years old. At least. On the fourth floor was an uncle. There had been no sign of him, but Luis warned he was the stereotypical crazy relative. Gabe wondered what meeting him would be like. He was grateful that he had the third floor to himself.

Although he'd expected it, the coldness of the place was a bit bland. It had all the coziness of a 1950s apartment in Communist Hungary. Plus, the concrete building offered very little in terms of amenities: no insulation, no HVAC system. Fortunately, there was running water, but it wasn't hot.

Gabe turned on the water in the kitchen sink. "No hot water?" Gabe said exasperated.

"Just in the bathroom. There's an electric heating system for that," Luis said.

"Right," Gabe said, remembering a similar situation from his last visit to Bolivia. Luis showed Gabe how to turn on the electric water heater at the showerhead.

Gabe stood bleary eyed and surveyed his new abode. The apartment was sixty feet long and ten feet wide, and in that six hundred square feet were a living room, kitchen, two bedrooms, and two bathrooms. The windows were all along one side. There was no refrigerator or microwave, not even a range. The last tenants had left a couple of beaten-up couches in the living room, and he was relieved to see that the main bedroom contained a bed. Nothing elaborate, but he figured he didn't need much. Just a place to crash and to store his stuff.

Luis helped Gabe move in and then they completed the lease—no mother-in-law required. It seemed odd to him that a lease was necessary, because if he left the country and went back to the US, he doubted the Bolivian government would try to extradite him for breaking the contract. Gabe was too exhausted to ask about it, and once his signature was on the paper, Luis rushed to depart.

Gabe stood in his new apartment alone faced with deafening silence. "Toto, we're not in Colorado anymore," he said aloud mimicking *The Wizard of Oz* line. No, he was living in an apartment in a completely different part of the world. He was in La Paz, in his new home, ready to positively impact the world. But before any of that, he really needed a shower and some sleep.

• • •

In Bolivia, most residential buildings lacked hot water heaters. Gabe was not alone in lacking the convenience most Americans have of hot water flowing on demand. In Bolivia as elsewhere, cold water enters from the street or a water storage container, which was usually found on the roof.

As Luis had pointed out, most shower heads in Bolivia are electrically charged. The shower head instantly heats up the water before it sprays down. A much different approach to a tankless water heater. The tip Gabe had learned on his first visit to Torotoro with his partners Nick and Michelle was that when the shower head was turned on and heating, he should avoid touching it. Otherwise, he'd get a shock. After hearing and learning about the water heating process, he very much took care not to touch the shower head while shampooing, soaping up, or rinsing. *Do. Not. Touch.*

Finally, out of his traveling clothes and ready to shed the germs and grime of the last thirty-five or so hours, he turned on the water heater and waited to step in until the room was filling with steam. Then he gingerly made his way under the water, carefully avoiding the shower head.

His yip could probably be heard by all his neighbors. This shower head somehow propelled the current down onto him all on its own. It was malfunctioning.

Maybe that's why Luis darted out of here so quickly after I signed the lease, Gabe thought.

He had two bathrooms, but only one had a shower. It was this or nothing. He gritted his teeth. All he wanted was to freshen up and relax.

Things seem like they're going to be so much harder here.

• • •

Amazing how an electrifying shower can restore energy to a tired traveler.

Wandering the streets of Sopocachi that evening, Gabe felt a little blue about his accommodations. But he tried to focus on the positive. *There's always an upside, right?* One advantage his building had over a lot of other ones he'd seen today: it was actually finished. Many others had clearly been abandoned after the concrete framing. Many had only three of four walls completed and no roofs. The buildings he'd walked by had been either old and decrepit or new and incomplete. His had all four walls and a roof.

He took note of the most appealing cafes because he was determined that after recovering from this day, he'd try one out. He hadn't learned enough Spanish for small talk, but surely he could speak enough of the language to purchase a coffee and maybe a dessert. He paused in front of one called the Alexander Café, steeled himself, and entered. The aroma was wonderful, and it was great to see people drinking their coffee and enjoying some small bites. He chose a table and sat. Mentally, he rehearsed the words for ordering a coffee, so by the time the waiter appeared, he had it down. The small cafe con leche and a piece of delicious cheesecake were a great end to the day.

Satisfied, Gabe shuffled back home to the apartment, wondering what all the other folks he was sitting next to in the coffee shop had been talking about, leading such seemingly normal lives. *Cities are strange,* he thought. *You're among millions of people, and yet can feel as alone as you might on a mountain.* Also, he concluded, when you don't speak the language, it's like there's a protective barrier between you and the rest of the living world.

The kids from downstairs were sitting on the front stoop, a soccer ball between them. They didn't budge.

"*Hola,*" Gabe managed.

They stared at him like he was from Mars, and then the older girl stood up to let him pass. Well, it was a start, anyway.

Upstairs, Gabe lay down on the bed, thinking about all the travel of the day, and he started drifting off. The bed was queen size, which was plenty big for him, and fairly comfortable. He was going to enjoy his first night of sleep on this new continent.

A loud *snap* jolted him awake and he found himself lying at a forty-five-degree angle looking at the wall. One of the wooden bars that stabilized the mattress had broken, and his bed was no longer flat.

For a second, he was convinced he was dreaming, or hallucinating like he might have been earlier with the zebras. It was dark, and his mind wasn't working at full capacity. But no, he wasn't dreaming. The bed was pitching sideways.

Slowly, he rolled off, trying not to break another crossbar. He would have to fix this bedframe before getting any sleep.

He found a hammer and some nails in the hallway closet, and somehow without nailing his thumb to the bed, he repaired the frame enough to be functional. But the result, unfortunately, wasn't great—the mattress was still far from flat. He'd just have to settle for a tilted bed. For now.

Thoughts cycled.

There are zebras wandering the streets.

My shower electrocutes me.

My bed tilts.

And he'd only been there twelve hours. Gabe was starting to realize that he might not have too many comfortable days and nights in Bolivia.

CHAPTER THIRTEEN
VANILLA SPRINKLED DONUTS

As it turned out, there were Alexander Cafés all around La Paz, and after Gabe had managed to order in one, he could now order food in the others. These cafes offered an escape as well as a treat, and it was good to have found a place where he could hang out in relative anonymity and blend in with the crowd.

June and July flew by. Gabe found his rhythm and his way around town. He got electricity and internet set up in his name and learned how to pay his month-to-month bills. He haggled with vendors buying a refrigerator and a range. He took buses and the trufis, which could be small cars or a van, to get anywhere he needed to go that he couldn't reach by walking. He eventually figured out what numbers the cashier at the grocery store meant when he checked out and was asked for them. At first, that had given him pause, but then a friendly English-speaking shopper explained that it was just something about taxes he was paying in Bolivia that as an expat he could get back later. He later left his debit card in an ATM and survived the minor catastrophe.

With thoughts of buying a small truck to use for scouting potential project sites, he ended up meeting a guy named Alejandro who had a truck to sell. Alejandro was personable and spoke decent English. He invited Gabe to join him and some friends for a coffee now and then. They even caught a few English-speaking movies. Alejandro was still in the late-night partying phase of life, so they weren't likely to be super tight, but it was great to have someone to connect with.

These minor successes and developments fueled Gabe's optimism. However, he was stymied about how to set up meetings with government officials. Email didn't work. Even if he could find a general email for inquiries, there was no one on the other end who ever replied. Stupefied, he decided to ask Ali. She had invited him over for dinner with her family, and he'd felt comfortable asking a few questions now and then.

Their apartment was a warm, inviting space in which Gabe immediately felt at home. They exchanged pleasantries and she introduced him to the family. Her husband was playing some kind of a board game with their young kids, so Ali invited him into the kitchen to chat as she finished up the last touches on the meal.

Gabe told her about some of his recent events and then explained he hadn't been able to set up meetings in the government because he couldn't contact people via phone or email.

"The infrastructure just isn't there," Ali said.

"Even in government offices?" Gabe asked, incredulous.

"Even in government offices," she said. "There are plenty of friendly employees there, but they don't rely on email the way you Americans do."

So Gabe wasn't just being rejected as some wacky person trying to make inroads. "Maybe I'll just show up," he said. "Walk in uninvited."

"Definitely," Ali said over her shoulder as she scooped quinoa from a pot into a serving bowl.

"I really need to have contacts in case we are scrutinized by anyone specific."

"Scrutinized?" Ali asked.

"Well, I've heard stories of nonprofits getting kicked out by officials. As in, the president."

"Ah. So you are worried about when Evo was newly in office and many organizations had to leave Bolivia. But I think you'll be okay. Things have settled down."

"Morales did promise to make walking right into government offices acceptable," Gabe said. "But I'm pretty sure he meant Bolivians, not random Americans."

Ali laughed. "Yes, but you are not shy."

In fact, Gabe had thought about meeting people by just walking through the hallways of government buildings and finding the right person or people he could talk to. Maybe he could do this.

"I wonder if bringing baked goods would help with engagement," he said.

Ali was placing steaming bowls and platters on the table. "Food never hurts," she said.

Indeed! Gabe knew how it broke down barriers when locals fed him. He had a plan.

• • •

On Monday, Gabe emerged from his apartment ready for his next journey. First, baked goods. He considered the bakery down the block that he loved, and then on a whim turned on his heel and walked several blocks in the other direction into a place he'd steered clear of called The Donut Factory. It had seemed too American in this period of immersing himself in everything Bolivian. But gut instinct told him that bringing something like donuts would make him memorable to any government employee he met that day.

As if his butchered Spanish wouldn't be enough for them to remember the American guy.

It worked. A box of vanilla sprinkled donuts was magic. Later, he discovered that cookies and other pastries were equally effective. *I guess the way to others' hearts really can be through their stomachs.*

When walking through the halls of the Ministry of Education, the Ministry of Rural Development, and the Ministry of Public Financing, Gabe would have his goodies in one hand and, in the other hand a one-pager explaining who he was, describing Pidola's projects, and listing their goals. Most times he didn't bring their interpreter with him since Lidy lived in Cochabamba.

Nothing says official business-like donuts. The connections Gabe made within these various departments worked so well that contacts in the US State Department occasionally asked Gabe to help them gather information. His access as a civilian was better—or at least different—from that which the diplomats could gain. They didn't want classified information, of course, just garden-variety information surrounding new hires, promotions, projects—things of that nature. So, he was like a little explorer finding his way around maze-like halls of government.

After some time Gabe had just two degrees of separation from Evo Morales himself, which he thought was pretty good considering his continuing lack of proficiency in Spanish and he was still in-country on a tourist visa. The relationships he established, especially within the Ministry of Education, were very fruitful.

From those initial conversations with people at the lowest levels of authority, to meeting with vice-ministers, Gabe made progress with building Pidola's reputation, as well as finding new project locations. It worked both ways, which of course was the idea. Representing Pidola, Gabe was there to help the ministries provide services and support for their citizens.

Still, the Ministry of Education's official stance was not to utilize outside entities to help with their programs. After just a few weeks of presentations, conversations, and a bit of negotiating Gabe entered into an unofficial agreement with them; it felt like a huge win, especially since he'd been in the country for only a few short weeks. They created a list of more than twelve hundred potential locations for Pidola's projects. It was great for the little organization, but also heartbreaking that there were thousands of other Pampa Jasis throughout the country, all needing the most basic resources.

During this time Gabe also finalized Pidola's newly formed entity in Bolivia, the equivalent of forming a new LLC in the United States. Nick, Michelle, and he had originally named their nonprofit Accendo Solutions, based on the Latin word *accendo*, which loosely translates into turn on or illuminate. Pidola loosely translated into *leapfrog*. The idea was that they'd be clearing two hurdles simultaneously, providing both renewable energy and the internet. They recycled the original name and called the Bolivian entity Accendo SRL.

Gabe would learn that it is a challenging process to start a company or nonprofit organization no matter where you live. It's an especially challenging experience when you start a company in another country, when you're not a citizen of that country, and when you don't know the laws, regulations, or requirements.

Looking back on all the hoops Gabe had to jump through at the beginning, he felt it was incredible that he'd completed that process at all. Most of the time he was just checking boxes, not knowing much about the steps he was taking to get this entity formed. He had essentially blindly signed papers that Pidola's lawyers—who earned and deserved his trust—put in front of him. And after two-and-a-half years from the initial idea of starting a nonprofit, he suddenly popped up, looked around, and was part owner of a Bolivian company negotiating agreements with the government.

Life is certainly not linear.

So now Gabe had Pidola's power of attorney, legal representation, and even an accountant and a public relations manager. Everything was aligning well. Now he just needed to raise the approximately twenty thousand dollars it would take to build another project. Minor detail.

CHAPTER FOURTEEN
THE YATIRI

Despite progress in some areas, Gabe started feeling worn. The novelties of being in a strange country were no longer shiny and new; the honeymoon with La Paz was coming to an end. Plus, he had a couple of situations that agitated him.

The first was at the local barber shop. He was not too particular about his hair that he was losing anyway. The risk of messing up a haircut wasn't a big deal. But he'd had his beard for the better part of ten years. So, when he entered the local barber shop and tried to explain what he was looking for in simple Spanish, it didn't end well. He had even rehearsed the conversation for an hour before he visited.

"*Corto a los lados, recorta la parte superior.*" Shorter on the sides, just a trim up top.

As he came to learn, so many things don't translate verbatim, and this was one of them. When the stylist looked at him like he had an arm coming out of his head, he knew she didn't understand him. Thankfully, she had pictures of models with various haircuts all over the walls, so he just pointed to the one closest to what he was looking for. Non-verbal became a big component in how he communicated. And Google Translate.

The haircut turned out fine, but the beard was an entirely different challenge. Not one of the men in the shop's posters had a beard. Most Bolivian men don't have facial hair, so beard trimming wasn't a special skill set any barber had. Gabe had shown her a picture of how he wanted his beard trimmed, but there was no chance. After she did a bit of shaping and trimming, the process went on to flat out trial and error, and his beard eventually disappeared. He felt like he was being petty or childish, but he was almost heartbroken. That beard had been with him for a long time. Emotional support facial hair. It had helped him connect with the children he'd met during his first trip to Bolivia. He reminded himself that the loss of a beard was a first-world issue, something superficial at best in poorer cultures; so many people around him lacked basic essentials.

The second situation concerned a trip he'd planned to climb Sajama. He knew that at some point he would be able to climb the peaks surrounding La Paz—Huayna Potosi, Illimani, etc., but he wanted to get to Sajama before the winter dry season ended. Sajama was about a four hour's drive from La Paz, and not only the highest peak in Bolivia, but also an undeniably beautiful one. A dormant stratovolcano, it stood over twenty-one thousand feet, heavily glaciated. It's conical and capped with a summit crater, a lonely but excellent contrast to its miles of flat surroundings. Gabe had seen pictures of it years before and had long been interested in climbing it. Plus, the weather was near perfect in Western Bolivia, so it sounded like a sure thing. He booked the trip with a local guide service to help with logistics.

In Bolivia and in many other Latin American countries, labor strikes were common and almost legendary. In some cases, they are downright dangerous and terrifying. Ali had told stories about the frequent strikes by miners who operated outside La Paz. When miners would enter the city to express their frustration for whatever reason, all the residents and local workers would leave. That was because the miners would detonate small amounts of dynamite right in downtown La Paz, which shook all the tall buildings nearby. Gabe would experience the effects of a strike firsthand.

After all of his plans of climbing Sajama were complete, a strike closed the main roads and entrances into the park. Hence, no one was allowed to enter Sajama National Park. For weeks, Gabe kept rescheduling the trip, but the climbing season window closed before the strike ended. Sajama would have to wait.

Such minor frustrations were starting to accumulate; something seemed to always be agitating Gabe. Coupled with the fact that his Spanish wasn't improving at the rate he had hoped, even after taking classes and practicing his Spanish every day for three months. Almost every interaction he had with anyone was stressful and annoying because he could barely understand what others were saying. He felt like he was getting nowhere. He couldn't even ask directions. Every financial transaction was difficult (*How much did that cost, again?*), every food order was incorrect (*Is this what I ordered?*). The positive trajectory of setting up Pidola's potential project locations was counterbalanced with the negative trajectory with both the lack of project funding and with his personal experiences. Gabe tried to remain positive and told himself repeatedly that the minor inconveniences and levels of discomfort he personally experienced were much less important than the work he was attempting to accomplish.

His mind knew that, but the rest of him felt otherwise.

• • •

One of the ways Gabe attempted to remain positive was to embrace the silly things he experienced. In La Paz, every day there was something uniquely eccentric—maybe even every hour. Some days he wouldn't even have to leave his apartment. For example, in Bolivia, and as he came to understand all throughout Latin America, some products and services actually came to you. Once a week, the "broom guy" blew his whistle as he walked down the street, selling his household item—thirty to forty brooms, in all different colors, in his backpack.

Same situation with services—for example, knife sharpening. Once a week, the "knife sharpener guy" blew his unique whistle—not to be confused with the broom guy's whistle—alerting everyone that he was in the neighborhood. Gabe found out later that most, if not all, knife sharpeners in Central and South America use the same whistle tone. If you had a dull knife, you just had to wait for the local guy to amble down your street. Same with propane, except they didn't whistle. A truck full of small propane tanks would blare its horn letting people know gas was for purchase. The propane truck couldn't be missed or mistaken.

Then there was the local high school marching band that would swing down the street practicing their songs.

All of that was colorful and delightful—most of the time.

But then came a sort of public health crisis—four weeks in which no garbage or trash was picked up anywhere in the entire city. At the primary landfill outside of La Paz, there had been a collapse of one of the major mountains of refuse. The pile was so big that a "trash-slide" demolished part of the road that led to the landfill, which meant trash trucks could not access it. No sense picking it up if there's nowhere to drop it off.

Although walking around the city had begun as a pleasant adventure, Gabe had to step over trash everywhere. He also carried a hiking pole to keep the wild dogs away. It was getting old, as was dodging wild, erratic drivers. He'd seen only four stop signs in the entire city. Two of them, he might have seen twice.

Catching a ride had also stopped feeling like a safe option. On more than one occasion, Gabe was pretty sure the cab driver was trying to kidnap him, or at least mug a naive tourist. *Why were we driving in the opposite direction than the way I wanted to go?* Multiple times he ended up throwing money at the driver and leaping out of the cab at the corner, only to walk home from the other side of La Paz. Sans hiking pole.

There was just enough chaos to keep things lively, not enough to make him *too* uncomfortable, and a growing list of tension-causing experiences. He tried to take it all in stride. And some of the more unique and interesting parts still elicited a smile.

• • •

That first day in La Paz with Luis driving, while he was still in a jet-lag daze, he thought he had seen a zebra on the street. Well, he had. He *knew* it! Zebras actually did roam the streets of both La Paz and El Alto. Well, not actual zebras. People in zebra costumes.

Any major Latin American city has immense levels of traffic congestion. Lima, Buenos Aires, Bogota, Mexico City. La Paz was no different, and the drivers' behavior could be downright criminal. At least compared to American road rules. To help ensure that pedestrians are safe when crossing the street, the city government employed people to help them navigate those crossing zones. In zebra costumes. The zebra pattern refers to the crosswalks' black-and- white stripes. These zebras were legendary. Not only did they help people cross busy city streets, but they were also minor celebrities who would take time for pictures with kids, tourists, and anyone else fascinated by them.

Gabe also heard that the city of La Paz employed other people to wear gorilla costumes and roam the neighborhoods and call out those making mistakes when crossing busy streets. They would show people what *not* to do as a pedestrian. Gabe had not yet seen a gorilla, but the story goes that occasionally fights would break out between the zebras and gorillas, mimicking a battle of right versus wrong. The zebras would always win, of course, as good in the end defeats evil.

• • •

Part of Gabe's struggle acclimating to life in Bolivia was that he lacked ways he had relied on at home in the US to decompress—no mindless, trash TV to wind down with (for him, that is, since most stations were in Spanish), and no Netflix or Amazon Prime. He had read all the books he'd brought. His favorite foods were four thousand miles away as were his favorite people. Climbing was no longer available due to finances and weather, and he had yet to connect with a church. There was really no one to really talk to. Discomfort, and now sorrow and loneliness were his constant company.

His inner voice lecturing him about lack of progress, he looked for small escapes. *I am in Bolivia and should take the opportunity for some cultural growth.*

Bolivia had dozens of indigenous peoples, one of which was the Aymara. In the Aymara culture, Yatiris read cocoa leaves to predict the future, like tarot card readers. One of his Spanish teachers knew a Yatiri. Her uncle. That sounded harmless enough.

Growing up Christian, Gabe had never put much stock in fortune telling, but he thought that this was a unique experience he shouldn't pass up. It was inexpensive. *What could it hurt? It may even be fun,* something he sorely needed.

Gabe arrived at an unassuming apartment building to meet Paola, who introduced him to her uncle. They walked up to the top floor of the four-story building, into a large, mainly empty living room; like always, the architecture gave Gabe the impression he was living in a Soviet Bloc country. He sat on a couch, facing a small coffee table where the Yatiri laid out a white tablecloth and threw down a couple of large handfuls of cocoa leaves. The way the leaves landed and piled up would tell what Gabe's future held. The Yatiri repeated the procedure a few times to ensure that what he was reading in the leaves was true. Gabe, who had a math mind, chuckled inside at the idea that the Yatiri wanted a significant sample size.

After a few moments of silence, the man shared his reading. With his teacher interpreting for him, Gabe learned he was to have a windfall of riches and that all his wildest dreams would come true.

The visit also allowed the Yatiri the chance to upsell Gabe for a *ch'alla*. For a cool three hundred and sixty-five dollars, Gabe could meet him in a spiritual setting outside of La Paz where he'd set a table on fire, which would facilitate going into more depth about fate. Given the results from the cocoa leaves reading, Gabe left well enough alone and took the positive news he already had back to his apartment. He figured he could set his own table on fire. At least his broken bed.

After that experience, Gabe realized it was time to find a church. That had always been a part of his life since childhood. It was through his church in Colorado that he'd ended up in Bolivia in the first place. Plus, church provided a community of like-minded people. With any luck, he'd make friends there—people who could get by in English enough to understand one another.

Luis was always on hand to be of help and was a great source of information about the culture and the city. And indeed, Luis had a church to recommend.

CHAPTER FIFTEEN

$4.34

Luis lived in the Los Pinos neighborhood of the Zona Sur, the southern area of La Paz. The area isn't far from Sopocachi—only about five or six miles, or two lines of a very enjoyable thirty-minute gondola ride. Gabe was familiar with Zona Sur. After visiting it on his very first day with Luis, he'd explored the neighborhood frequently and felt at ease there, especially since Pidola's lawyers and other partner organizations were in that part of town.

Sunday mornings, Gabe hopped on the gondola line at eight-thirty, then walked three miles to the church for the ten o'clock service. Because he was watching every *centavo* and the taxis and *trufis* were more expensive, the Teleferico was his mode of transport. When he wasn't riding the cable car system, he walked. Everywhere. Sundays were no different.

Gabe had gone to church with his family every weekend while growing up, and later in life he found great church communities in other places where he lived. Even though Pidola was not a faith-based organization, he and his partners' efforts were furthering God's work. Gabe strongly believed that alignment was more than just a coincidence. He was convinced that God had given him this great opportunity to do good work for people in need.

The people were welcoming within the church in Los Pinos. Some spoke a little English, and they were eager to learn why Gabe had moved to La Paz, and what he was doing there. Very few foreigners made their way to this church, so as an outsider he was a bit of an attraction, the object of some attention. Since conversations were a blend of Spanish and English—neither party was ever fully sure they were understanding the other, but Gabe made the best of it.

• • •

No matter where Gabe had lived in the US, the Christian services he attended all seemed similar. In a Bolivian church, the passion and energy were way more enthusiastic, more so than anything he had ever experienced—at least at this little church in the south of La Paz.

Each Sunday the small basement-level room was always packed; some people would even sit on the steps leading down into the main congregation area. The people seemed to sing louder, the pastor preached with more conviction and animation, the way Gabe imagined a Southern Baptist or Evangelical minister might. Attending weekly didn't change the fact that he still didn't understand most of what the pastor was saying. Yet, the spirited environment of this community validated to Gabe the importance of religion to Bolivianos, that it was a central part of their culture and society. It was always present, and for Gabe provided a familiarity and comfort that had been missing.

Religion had always been part of Gabe's support system. After his siblings and he reached adulthood, they all continued to attend church wherever they lived. Gabe's father even played the role of substitute pastor from time to time. With the opportunity to do some great work on a grand scale through his nonprofit, Gabe felt that God and he were finally singing from the same hymn sheet. He was opening the doors, and Gabe was walking through them.

• • •

It was soon after that, in late September and early October, that the balance he so tried to achieve in his life titled toward the negative as a wave of unexpected costs hit Gabe one after another.

The condo Gabe was renting out at home needed a few repairs: a new air handler, a new dishwasher, an unexpected HOA assessment involving new sidewalks in the community. It was becoming death by a thousand financial cuts.

Gabe had moved to Bolivia with a bit of savings, but now he was coming to the realization that he was woefully unprepared for unanticipated expenses. Money, as his father always told him, *was* "easy to spend, and hard to make," and that Colorado property was draining him. With his savings dwindling exponentially faster than he could replenish them, he was getting *really* nervous. In late October, Gabe checked his bank account and saw that he had less than five dollars to his name. His part-time income covered only his immediate living costs in Bolivia. Financial blows can be emotionally depleting to anyone, and this one came at a time when Gabe had very little mental and emotional reserve left.

His only credit card was maxed out, and with such a modest income, there was no way he could get approved for another one. He was suddenly like the people around him, barely squeaking by and mounting concern about how to make even the most basic ends meet. His inability to cope emotionally again reinforced the notion that life in the US had been too easy.

He thought of those families in America struggling to subsist making minimum wage. Gabe finally understood the reality of standing next to a financial cliff. *How did people get by?* He was making twice what someone making minimum wage in the States, yet he was nearly destitute. Racked with self-pity, he regretted ever buying a latte or treating himself to a meal.

He felt guilty that he felt so miserable, a negatively reinforcing cycle. *So many people, and most all over the world, live on so much less.* This crisis was teaching him a valuable lesson, he knew, and some invaluable humility. But at that moment, it just felt awful.

In only four weeks after visiting the Yatiri, he concluded that the prophecy of discovering endless riches was dead wrong. Instead of a windfall, he was on the verge of bankruptcy.

Despite still attending church, Gabe delighted in his now reinforced appreciation for people who found joy, not in material goods, but in family, tradition, and spirituality.

CHAPTER SIXTEEN
NOTHING LIKE FAMILY

Gabe had only been there for four months, but having always been hard on himself, he questioned his abilities to accomplish his goals—particularly on the fundraising end. Sure, he'd made progress setting up some of Pidola's operations, but he was getting nowhere fast on finding the needed money. Not one corporation, NGO, or government organization wanted to fund Pidola for a variety of reasons. Chief among them was that Pidola was too small or unproven, it wasn't in their budget this year, and the market was challenging. None of the hundreds of applications and letters of interest were accepted; many didn't even send replies. It was the classic chicken-and-the-egg scenario. The question was starting to creep into

Gabe's head: *What if it was a mistake moving to Bolivia?*

Fortunately, in mid-October, his mom and aunt arrived for a visit. The distraction from his troubles couldn't have been better timed.

When Gabe had told his family he was moving to Bolivia for a year, his mom and aunt instantly said they were coming to visit. Aunt Marilyn was an avid traveler and always wanted to see and experience a new part of the world, and Lake Titicaca was on his mom's bucket list. It was perfect timing. A win-win-win.

When Gabe met them at the airport, it was all he could do *not* to have a full breakdown right there at the baggage claim. The relief of seeing them and the safety he felt in their company opened his emotional floodgates. It took all his strength to hold them shut, gathering his strength to compose himself, telling himself that this time with family was going to be just what the doctor ordered.

His mom and aunt needed to acclimatize to the altitude, so everyone took it slow those first couple of days. Gabe's family had always loved playing cards, so they played many rounds of rummy and Phase 10. It was so comforting, as if home had arrived in La Paz.

Once they were ready to venture out, Gabe guided them to all the typical, most popular sites. The Witches Market was a total tourist trap but a must-see when visiting La Paz—the aphrodisiac formulas, wild Aymaran costumes, and dried-out llama fetuses. They had dinner with Luis, introducing the family to standard Bolivia fare.

After those first lazy days, Gabe started to feel better. Just being able to have a conversation in English was a huge relief, let alone hearing about life and his family back in the US. He focused on showing them Bolivia and had no time to listen to his pesty, insatiable inner voice.

Gabe's mom and Aunt Marilyn's favorite activity in La Paz ended up being to ride the gondolas of the Teleferico. Gabe showed them all dozen or so different service lines, each carrying hundreds of cabins, all looking down from above on the city streets and buildings. Not only is the cable car an easier way to get around, especially during times of heavy traffic, but also the gentle swaying on the Teleferico were relaxing, almost therapeutic. Gabe loved the Teleferico and was happy to ride it as a tour guide to his mom and aunt. They took the gondolas all over town—up to El Alto and to the city's flea markets, down to Calacoto and Zona Sur, and over to the historic General Cemetery.

The first few days passed, and both his mom and Aunt Marilyn had acclimatized well. They were ready for their first adventure, Lake Titicaca.

• • •

Driving up into and out of El Alto, the snow-capped and glaciated peaks of the Cordillera Real range could be seen to the right of the road. On the left, there was the vast emptiness of the high plains that didn't end until reaching the upper Andes and the desert volcanoes of Chile. Sajama, too. The day of their journey was crystal clear, and they could see dozens of miles in all directions as they approached Lake Titicaca. After a few hours on the road and a quick ferry across a narrow part of the lake, they entered the town of Copacabana, a small, quintessential South American town of about six thousand people. They stayed only briefly since they were on their way to Isla del Sol, which is in the middle of the lake.

Lake Titicaca was impressive, the type of place that pictures could not do justice.

Their small group, which included a tour guide, hopped on a small speed boat that would take about two hours to get to Isla del Sol, giving them time to make small talk and take in the scenery. In the lulls in the conversation, Gabe gazed peacefully at their surroundings. Looking to the north and east, he saw the on-going mountains, with Illampu jutting out, almost guarding them and the lake itself. He wondered if he would be fortunate enough with the opportunity to climb that peak down the road. To the south and west, there were vistas of the enormous lake that met the horizon, with sporadic breaks of hills and the smaller hills and peaks of Peru.

Gabe snuck peeks at his mom and aunt to make sure they were traveling well. With the rocking and constant hum of the boat's engine, his aunt fell into a hard sleep. His mom, on the other hand, was very much present and soaking it all in.

Gabe thought about the importance of being in the moment, especially in our go-go life in America. Pausing our incessant multitasking to just be present is so good for a person. Buddhists, yogis, and self-help, mindfulness gurus alike preach the benefits of letting go of the constant churn of thoughts about the past or the future to just be. *It's incredible to witness someone do it,* Gabe thought while observing his mother. *Wish I could.*

Gabe's mom was totally in the moment, soaking in every bit of her bucket list experience of being on the lake and heading toward Isla del Sol. It was obvious. She was just *there*, embracing the now. Gabe guessed he was fully present, too. He felt a peace than he had not felt in weeks—maybe months. Maybe since arriving in Bolivia.

If nothing else, at least for the briefest of moments, he was able to give someone else something important. Because he was living there, his mom was seeing a place she'd always wanted to visit. Gabe was the reason she'd come to northwest Bolivia and was surrounded by the beauty of one of the most impressive places in the world.

• • •

A week later, the three of them took the forty-five-minute flight from La Paz to Uyuni, a small town about one hundred miles southwest of La Paz in the southern part of the high plains of Bolivia. The town of Uyuni was adjacent to the world's largest salt flats, one of the three most visited tourist destinations in Bolivia.

Gabe hadn't given the salt flats much thought. He was still interested in visiting Sajama National Park, especially since by then the strikes had ended. But there would be time for that later. For now, he felt pleased that his guests had chosen that destination, a place he would not have ventured to on his own. Visiting the ancient lakebed would provide Gabe with an even deeper appreciation of just how extraordinary the country was.

They made their way from the small prop plane to find their next guide, who picked them up in a typical Toyota 4Runner. More time to soak up the scenery, which was mountainous on the right with vast plains to the left. They saw the occasional vicunas—Bolivia's equivalent of the North American deer—and various species of birds they couldn't identify. Then the group caught a glimpse of the beginnings of the salt flats far in the distance.

The flats are exactly that—big, old, flat, salt beds. They're nothing much by definition. But once in the middle of them, they were undeniably beautiful. The scale, the vastness of these dried lake beds was so dramatic, especially against the blue skies, and brown and white mountains in the far distance, that Gabe and his guests found them breathtaking. Driving in from the edge, the guide pointed them straight into the middle of the complete openness of the flats. The lakebed where the flats formed is so big that, like at Lake Titicaca, the horizon in all directions ended in white. How the guide knew where to navigate was beyond Gabe; he just knew. He drove almost into the middle of the expansive white, which could only be compared to an alien landscape. There are very few places like it on earth. The ground gave the illusion that it was covered in snow—but it was salt.

Overwhelming appreciation for this location struck Gabe as he stood in the middle of one of the world's most beautiful places. There, in Uyuni, he was as present as his mom had been on that boat on Lake Titicaca. There was magic in Uyuni.

This small, relatively unknown, land-locked country of Bolivia had so much for people to see and do. Gabe had learned and understood how amazing the people were, and now he was fully appreciating its natural beauty as well. *So much of this country is a treasure,* he thought. He was overwhelmed with gratitude that he'd been able to discover it and, through his work, to become a part of it.

The three of them spent only a couple of days in the salt flats, but none of them would ever forget it. As Gabe had no expectations, similar to when planning a climb, he was surprised by the magnificence of the place, and it was even better because he never would have placed it on his list. What a beautiful accident.

• • •

After flying back to La Paz, Gabe's mom and aunt had only a few more days in Bolivia. Out came the cards. Dozens of games of rummy again soothed his soul.

Gabe's family was not an overly expressive one, but he could see in his mom and his aunt's faces the joy they'd experienced visiting Bolivia and having time together. He felt tranquil with them around, more than they could ever have known.

It was impossible for him to describe the sense of loneliness he experienced when they boarded their plane back to the US. That day, they'd taken a gondola one last time, and Gabe dropped them off at the airport where they said their goodbyes. He was hopeful that he'd see them over Christmas, but given his current financial strife, he inwardly had some doubts. He didn't let them know how bad things were financially; like many families, they didn't like to make one another worry. But when he saw them off and onto the plane, all the problems and issues that he was facing before they visited rushed into the vacuum left in their wake. His fears were staring at him once again and he couldn't look away.

Gabe had no money, Pidola's funding was non-existent, and he was questioning what he was doing in Bolivia. Now that his family was gone, it hit him like a sack of potatoes. He was completely alone—of his own doing—and now it felt worse than before they arrived. He'd remembered the joy of being among people he loved.

On an hourly, maybe minute-by-minute basis, the thoughts revolved. *What the hell am I doing here?*

His family heading back to the US made Gabe realize how much he had left behind, and how isolated and exposed he was making himself. Nothing was working as intended. After all his careful planning before moving to La Paz to live, he was experiencing that firsthand.

By early November, Gabe felt that he had reached rock bottom, or so he thought. Little did he know that he was about to be completely stripped down and face to face with what he would come to realize was the worst version of himself.

CHAPTER SEVENTEEN
COOKIE MONSTER PAJAMA BOTTOMS

Gabe wasn't a big guy. When he left Colorado, he stood five-eight and a decently lean one hundred and fifty pounds. By the end of December 2018, he had lost nearly twenty percent of his body weight. He was turning into skin and bones.

It certainly didn't help that the water had stopped flowing through the pipes of La Paz.

Some issues just seem to take longer to resolve in South America than they do in the States. Gabe had learned that a few months earlier when his trash removal was suspended for a few weeks. Somewhere along the city's water lines a pipe had burst, rendering half of the city and three hundred thousand residents without water. Gabe's apartment was one of the affected buildings, and the water was out for close to a week.

On the first day of the water outage, he wasn't too concerned about getting by. He was one of the lucky ones who could shower, because he belonged to a gym close by that hadn't been affected. He was grateful for *all* the facilities there. Also, he was able to purchase bottled water for brushing his teeth, making some coffee, etc. He was learning to adjust.

Sidewalk vendors in the neighborhood were so inexpensive that Gabe, even in his desperate financial state, could afford a few modest meals out. A small Mexican place next to Abaroa Plaza had caught his eye, and one night he splurged on a burrito for dinner. Burritos were an all-time favorite of Gabe's and a staple for climbers and hikers—inexpensive and high in calories.

However, a few hours later, he knew he had made a mistake. Lying in his bed, he felt stomach pains that only grew worse as the night went on. Sweating profusely, curled up in a ball, he knew exactly what was coming. He'd had food poisoning before, and he now had it from the meal he'd just eaten.

Before long, he felt so sick that irrational thoughts mushroomed. He imagined seeking help from the police. *If I could just get to the entrance to the police station on the corner of my block and lie down, the first officer who arrived could take me to the hospital.*

For the next week, the effects of food poisoning kept Gabe from any meetings in the city and away from his daily Spanish classes. Close to home base. All this without water. At least there was the Teleferico station that was only five blocks away and for whatever reason had a bathroom with running water. It must have been a sight for the neighbors to see: the strange white dude waddling to the public toilets multiple times a day. His brother had given him Cookie Monster pajama bottoms years before, and for a few of those five-block waddles, he was wearing Muppet pants. The bathroom attendant must have thought he was a total weirdo when he gave him his allotted one square of toilet paper.

Yes. One square.

The first time he was handed that meager square, he passive aggressively, in English, said, "Are you fucking serious?" The attendant couldn't understand him, of course, so he could just let his frustration out by cursing the poor guy. After that, he brought his own.

One of the very Bolivian things Gabe learned during his time in La Paz was that geography mattered. Whether it be how much or little rain your community received, or if you were close to a river that was going to get dammed for hydroelectric power, location was important. For La Paz, local farms provided the city supermarkets and street vendors fruits and vegetables. But these farms were located *downstream*, where all the city's runoff went. That same water was used for irrigation. Gabe didn't think too much of it until he learned that La Paz didn't have a water treatment plant. Hence, anyone unaccustomed to the local water and bacteria was susceptible to getting sick. He had just been lucky up to that point in time.

As he began to feel better, Gabe started checking, and double checking, his food. It became an obsession. He scrutinized expiration dates on various products in the supermarket, and noticed for the first time that many items should have been removed from the shelves. He found a box of cereal that had an expiration date of a year ago. He once bought a loaf of bread only to discover at home that the entire center of it was moldy. Bacon well past its prime. Then he learned that supermarkets sold many expired products to local street vendors, who in turn scratched off the expiration dates and resold them. No place was safe. He started to appreciate the infrastructure and regulations in the US more and more.

Two weeks later, he found himself sick again. Whether it was some sort of relapse, or another bout of food poisoning, he couldn't be sure, but at least the water had been restored, and he didn't have to scurry to the Teleferico station bathroom.

Gabe was losing almost a pound of weight a day and ended up being on the wrong side of one hundred and thirty pounds, a weight he hadn't seen since his teenage years. He was trying to eat all he could, but he wasn't able to keep weight on. For the first time in his life, he was worried about just surviving. As a climber, he'd had some frightening moments in the mountains from time to time, but this was a first when not in the wilderness. He had a feeling that he was going to die by withering away. He had thought about just showing up at the local hospital, but he wasn't familiar with the system. Especially if any costs were going to be out-of-pocket.

Then, he remembered that he had brought an antibiotic often used by mountain climbers in the wilderness. After a week of taking the medicine, he seemed to finally be back on the mend.

But by then, the damage had been done, and he was now also so mentally and emotionally unwell that he was seriously frightened. His isolation and loneliness peaked. He'd failed to keep up the friendship with Alejandro and he didn't feel comfortable calling on Luis for help—he had his own family to worry about, and besides, he was a colleague. Now Gabe was also psychologically at the end of his rope, stricken by a feeling of overwhelming failure.

Seeking more meaning had come, in part, from his inability to build a family life at home. And now, he was confronted with the notion of being regarded as a failure in this effort, too. His inner voice was screaming.

What would all the people back home think of me now? I moved here to make this nonprofit work, and I have failed. I'd have to crawl home with my tail between my legs.

His mind kept circling back to the same question he'd asked himself many times over the past six months and again after his mom and aunt had left: *What the hell am I even doing here anymore? I have no money, and no new projects are even close to being started.*

He prayed that things would turn the corner, but every new day seemed worse than the previous one. Even his spirituality, which had been his anchor for as long as he could remember, was in question. He had been praying to no avail and thought, *Now, where is God? Didn't we have an understanding, an agreement, that if I would move to Bolivia, we'd push forward all this good work? Where is He?* Gabe felt abandoned.

To add to the misery, soon he would be turning forty, a time when people often question the arc of their lives. He felt loveless, hopeless, and purposeless, and was totally ashamed of it all, including of his depressed feelings. He had no idea it was clinical depression—and the poor perspective he was experiencing just made things worse.

With the people he still regularly spoke to back in the US, he didn't want to talk about his situation. It was all too embarrassing. It was easy to hide how he was feeling from friends and family thousands of miles away. By December, he was in such a dissociative state of mind and body that he was by no means thinking clearly.

Even though Gabe had lived through tough times before, his depression and melancholy had been far less severe, and he was able to persevere without medical attention. Now, his undiagnosed and untreated depression left him at the end of everything. He wasn't alive, he wasn't dead. He'd never imagined life could be so hollow.

All he had wanted to do was to make the world a better place. Now, it felt like all he had really accomplished was destroying himself.

• • •

Gabe once heard a story from his Uncle Steve about a time when he was on the Kali Gandaki River, a popular river for whitewater rafting in Nepal. As anyone who has rafted this river knows, it's gnarly, with class III, IV, and V whitewater.

The story goes that while his uncle was rafting, he was thrown into the water and ended up *under* the raft. After struggling for a time, he came to realize that he wasn't going to be able to find the surface. Gabe's uncle became certain that he was going to die right then and there. When he was telling Gabe this story, he'd said, "I felt at ease, I felt at peace, and I was calm knowing that this was how I was going to die."

While hearing the story, Gabe didn't think much of those comments. Of course, his uncle didn't die. He was right there in front of Gabe. But thinking back on what he'd said, Gabe now realized what a remarkable experience his uncle was describing. To be right on the edge, to stop fighting, and to still be able to come back, was extraordinary. In the end, his guide pulled him out and Gabe was sure that experience changed his Uncle Steve's perspective.

Now, Gabe thought a lot about this story and the peace his uncle had found on the Kali Gandaki. He too was beginning to feel that peace. He believed his time had come, and he was fine with it.

• • •

During Gabe's first six months in Bolivia, he had made a short trip to Cochabamba to meet with some potential partner organizations. Ever since the first time the three Pidola founders had gone to Cochabamba, they'd always stayed at the same hotel right downtown—the Toloma

Gran Hotel. Gabe hadn't thought too much about it then, but they had been on the top floor, which was more than a hundred feet above the street. For whatever reason, he had opened a window and thought it strange that the window opened all the way. In the US, many hotel windows only open a crack, so children can't fall out of them.

Now, having reached the conclusion that he'd had enough, he remembered that moment, that open window, that one-hundred-foot drop. Gabe thought that the next time he was in Cochabamba, maybe he would get a room on the top floor of the Toloma Gran Hotel—and step out. *What's the point anymore?* His place and purpose were nonexistent. He was causing more harm than good at this point.

Gabe of course knew that literal step would hurt his family and his friends, and certainly would make a mess for the Cochabambinos. But he was at the *very* bottom and not thinking clearly. He lacked perspective, gratitude and was unable to see that he was loved. He was taught to think that taking one's life is the ultimate selfish act, but he felt that doing so would ultimately spare himself the pain and suffering of dealing with his failure. Maybe the next time he was in Cochabamba would be his last.

Fortunately, Gabe couldn't get to Cochabamba. He didn't have enough money in the bank or available credit on his card to get there. Being on the brink of bankruptcy had destroyed him emotionally, but, ironically, it was keeping him in place and alive.

CHAPTER EIGHTEEN
MAGIC AT THE BOTTOM

In mid-December, Gabe was on the phone with Michelle talking about their plans for the upcoming Christmas holiday. He finally mentioned, for the first time—to anyone—that he was broke and therefore wasn't coming back for the holidays.

By that point, Michelle knew Gabe well. They'd been friendly colleagues and had become close friends while working on the foundations of Pidola. They'd been through the highs and lows together for the Pampa Jasi project; thick and thick. She sensed that something was seriously wrong and declared that he needed to get back home to see family and friends. To get away from it all. She told him it was time to take a break from Bolivia. Then she said, "And I'm paying for your ticket."

There was no room for argument. Little did she know, with that incredible gesture, she may have been saving Gabe's life.

Because of Michelle's kindness, Gabe was able to fly home to see family and friends in both Pennsylvania and Colorado for Christmas and New Year's, where everyone who cared about him could see where he was both physically and emotionally. One friend came right out and said, "Dude, you're definitely on the pain train." Gabe didn't discuss with anyone the extent of the situation or the depth of the pain he was experiencing, but it was painted all over his face, and his body language spoke louder than words.

While Gabe was back in Philadelphia for Christmas, he ended up having dinner with one of his oldest and closest friends. Gabe cracked the door open just a bit and spoke about the last couple of months before the holiday. And reflected.

"You know, I have a feeling, and not just a fleeting, glancing feeling. It's something deep down, something visceral. That what I'm going through right now, and have been over the last few months, that this is important."

"Why? What's making you think and feel that way?", his friend asked back.

"Maybe there's magic at the bottom. Like my canvas is getting wiped clean. That I'm getting stripped down to the studs, to the bare metal. Maybe it's time where I can rebuild myself into a more aware person, a more compassionate person."

His friend replied, "Yes, compassion for others has never been an issue for you. You're very altruistic. But you also need to take care of yourself as well."

"I think I have hit bottom because I don't see how things could be worse," Gabe lamented. "I feel like a failure in every respect. There is no peace in my life, just embarrassment."

"Gabe. Did you ever think that this all might be a test of your resolve and fortitude? That maybe this time in your life is a blessing in disguise. That maybe it's a gift, a chance for you to reboot your life and perspective? You feel like a failure because of how you perceive others will judge you. Forget about everyone else."

"So, you think that my experience in South America may actually lead to something positive? I mean, I get it, but I just can't see it or feel it. "No one ever redefines oneself when feeling content. No one ever stops to change one's life when participating in the rat race, running at top speed. Maybe this experience will make me slow and understand why I feel so broken. Time for some reframing. There has to be message here."

"Gabe, it's common for people to talk and work towards the better version of themselves. This could be your time."

"But maybe it's also important to find the worst version, too."

Gabe said. "Can someone really find the best without knowing the worst? Maybe this is my stress test and that I just need to own and lean into all of this. I mean, I have no place to hide down there, I just need to dig in and work the problem."

Gabe pondered his friend's words for days and, as he sorted through them, began to sense a clarity in thought instead of the muddle of the punishing, self-deprecating thoughts that had seemed unrelenting. He eventually thought, with a glimmer of hope, that it was time to accept it all and heal. Maybe the pendulum had swung to its most extreme point and was finally getting back to center. He thought of another nugget of wisdom his friend had bestowed.

"The foundation of who you fundamentally are never really disappears. If you can and are lucky enough, though, you may find the chance to wipe that foundation clean and rebuild yourself as you like, better than before. In order to gain anything, you have to first lose everything." His friend replied with a quote from Jane Hirshfield." More words of wisdom from his friend as they parted ways after dinner.

As Gabe slowly began to recover from the despair and depression that had crashed over him, he thought it would take the rest of his life to appreciate what had happened to him. Instead, it was to take three painful years of self-reflection and self-exploration.

• • •

Gabe could have stayed home in Colorado and left Bolivia in Bolivia. Some would say he should have stayed home. But it was the promise he'd made to his co-founders that got him back onto the plane to La Paz. He'd promised them he'd give it a year to get operations set up and situated, and he didn't want to break that promise. *I am a man of my word. At least I have that.*

Even if there was the smallest and faintest opportunity, he wanted to give it everything he had to bring these projects to life. Maybe not twelve hundred sites, as he'd dreamed, but with just one or two more, he could hold his head up high and be proud of what he had accomplished. He told himself that all the pain and suffering he was experiencing would be worth it.

So, he got back on a plane in January 2019, heading back to La Paz, bruised, battered, numb, terrified, and nearly lifeless. He was starting with a completely new canvas to work with.

Jokingly, he thought, *At least on this trip I will have more than one pair of pants.* the one bit of good news was that at least he had more than one pair of pants.

CHAPTER NINETEEN
FRENCH BALLERINA

Three weeks in the US had been therapeutic. Spending time with family and friends helped improve his state of mind and allowed him to ultimately get back onto the plane.

Gabe knew he needed to find ways to keep his head on straight while pushing through the second half of his time in Bolivia. He knew two things that would help him get started. Getting back to the basics.

One of his secondary reasons for moving to Bolivia had been climbing. The dry season in the central Andes was right around the corner, starting in late April. Over Christmas, he had finalized plans with his brother Larry for a visit in May, and Sajama National Park would be part of that trip. Instead of visiting Sajama twice in six months, he eyed another peak—Illimani.

Illi is "the" peak outside of La Paz, visible from the city on a clear day and dominating the landscape south of town. It hovers over the city, resembling a royal crown, with four glaciated peaks running north and south. At well over twenty-one thousand feet, Illi was a great mountain for people training for the taller peaks in the Himalayas and the highest peaks at over 8,000 meters. Illi was not super technical, but could at times be demanding, requiring skill and focus. So, for the next four months, Gabe would have to train properly for Illi, and find a very inexpensive guide service.

As Gabe had learned while developing his mountaineering skills at the Colorado Mountain Club, training to attempt big mountains was painful and the regimens could be similar to those for running ultra-marathons or a triathlon. But the physical demands of climbing were almost inhumane. Not only do climbers need to be fit enough to hike up and down a mountain, but they also needed to be able to carry forty pounds of gear for thousands of feet of elevation gain and for numerous days on end. Rope, food, clothing, mountaineering axes, crampons, and lots of other bits and pieces of gear were required. Mountaineers carry their lives on their back.

Then there's the altitude. The great equalizer. Altitude is something you really can't train for. Sure, there are such things as hypoxic chambers, and spending enough time at altitude to acclimatize. But nothing perfectly mimicked the conditions on the mountain. Gabe was surely better positioned than usual for altitude stress because he was sleeping at twelve thousand feet above sea level every night. But he knew that altitude affects *everyone* differently on each attempt. Even if he typically felt good and strong at high altitudes, he could always have a bad day. Scaling high summits was dangerous, not only for the climber, but also for the team around him.

Despite his awareness of these tremendous mental and physical demands, Gabe couldn't wait to get onto Illi. He felt motivated, energized, alive.

One of the aspects of mountaineering that originally drew Gabe in was the demands of the sport, both physical and mental. It took complete dedication and concentration, stressing his body for the pure enjoyment of reaching the summit. And that's if you *reach* the summit. Many times, climbers have to abandon their attempts, so add disappointment to the challenge. The sport was both masochistic and hedonistic. Gabe thought of an adage within the mountaineering community describes it best: *"It's not the mountain you conquer, it's yourself."*

And that's what Gabe loved about the sport. Each time he climbed, there was a cautious mindset of how hard he could push himself. How much could he handle? How could he push past his personal comfort thresholds? How much could he grow? These are the things everyone learns about themself on the mountain and takes back into the real world. Gabe knew that each time he'd come back a better person for it. And that's what he needed now. Summit or not.

Maybe I should incorporate this mindset into all life's challenges?

In all of human history, there's probably never been a situation in which actually reaching the summit of a mountain was required for survival. Crossing difficult ranges, sure, but not reaching the formidable peaks that dominate a landscape and inspire human imagination. When considering the mental and spiritual growth gained from mountaineering, Gabe saw it as both a worthy endeavor and a beautiful thing.

He thought of something Nietzsche had written: *"Those who were seen dancing were thought to be insane by those who could not hear the music."* Gabe was ready to dance to the music again.

• • •

Training started almost as soon as he got off the plane in early January. Weight training at the gym would, of course, be a part of the regimen, as well as some bouldering at the local climbing club. At the time, in all of Bolivia there were a total of three climbing gyms. Fortunately, one of those gyms was only two blocks away from his apartment. Some might take that as a sign. But most of the time and energy spent training for Illi would be throughout the streets of La Paz.

The first Saturday morning that he was back in La Paz, Gabe started "working the big bag," a term he adopted from boxers for the training that involves walking around with a hiking backpack filled with bags of sand. Initially, he'd throw a twenty-five-pound bag of sand into the backpack, and eventually work his way up to fifty pounds to replicate the weight of gear needed for the climb.

The gentleman at the hardware store looked at Gabe like he had three heads when he asked for bags of sand. Few tourists or expats visited his store looking for, well, much of anything, let alone bags of sand. But Gabe procured them and dragged them home.

Those first few weekends, he carried the smaller bag of sand, a bottle of water, and a small snack. His training walks began at the Pata Obrajes Teleferico station at just over ten thousand feet above sea level and followed the yellow transit line to the last station in El Elto at around thirteen thousand feet. The trip was just short of four miles, and every time involved a new experience.

Everyone Gabe passed gave him a curious look—often a snicker. Hikers with backpacks were not common on the streets of La Paz. Actually, neither were people out for pleasure strolls. Who wanted to expose themselves to all those vehicle fumes for no apparent reason? Since auto emissions testing didn't exist in Bolivia, most of Gabe's two-hour training involved sucking down smoke from the clunkers all over the roads. Curious as to what on earth he was doing, onlookers probably also had a bit of disgust. A foreigner was doing something totally inessential and inconsequential; this project would have no effect on anyone but Gabe. The selfishness.

At the beginning, Gabe would start out by passing the presidential palace, which he realized was insanely accessible to the general public compared to the levels of security at the White House or even state capital buildings. The palace was almost like any other building in La Paz, other than the two security guards standing out front. Yes, two.

Next, he'd pass behind the US Embassy, where he would be spending more time later that year, but he had no vision of that yet as he trained in the streets. After about an hour in, the hard part began.

Near the second-to-last Teleferico station on the yellow line, Quta Uma, Gabe would take a break to drink water and eat his snack, usually a protein bar, and get ready for the nearly vertical remainder of the trek. That's where the most difficult and dangerous aspects of the training "hike" were, both what he would encounter and whom. After the Quta Uma station was a small park, an unofficial trail people used for their daily activities. Almost every time, he was harassed by a group of unruly drunks or unfriendly teenagers hanging out. He had no idea if they were harmless or if they'd have no hesitation mugging a clueless American.

Things looked more ominous at dusk, so he took most of his walks in the morning. After a few weeks of seeing the same groups, especially the drunks just waking up from the night before, he got more comfortable with them, and they did with him—the intruder on their territory became a known quantity. A harmless one.

One day, a few of the guys in the older group Gabe would regularly encounter asked him where he was from. As the conversation progressed, the oldest of the group mentioned something that made Gabe pause. Was this another comment that he didn't understand in Spanish? Could the guy have possibly just said, "*Solía ser bailarina en Francia?*"

Did he just say that I am a ballerina from France?

Gabe was almost certain that's what the man said.

I'll take that as a good sign that he's comfortable with me, Gabe thought as he smiled.

The second part of the trek, and the final push of Gabe's weekly training, was through the neighborhood passed through before reaching the flat part of El Alto. Past the streets of Julio Tellez and Calle 8 de Mayo, this area of the city was at its most vertical. Gabe had done enough snow climbing in Colorado's couloirs, snow gullies, so he had a pretty good idea of vertical degrees, and he knew these steps were at least a fifty-degree gradient. He passed one- and two-room brick houses there that had small yards in which vegetables grew and chickens roamed. Gabe carried a hiking stick, since there were stray dogs *everywhere*. Many times, due to the angle at which he was climbing up the neighborhood steps, he and a dog would surprise each other by ending up face-to-face. More than once, he had to shoo away an aggressive canine with his hiking pole. He couldn't be sure if it was the bag on his back or the now regrown beard on his face, but most dogs didn't like him. Perhaps they, like the drunks and teens, also found him a suspicious intruder on their turf.

This area is great for training but more life threatening than climbing a glaciated peak, Gabe chuckled nervously as he passed a snarling canine.

For the next four months, every weekend, Gabe took the same route, saw the same people, and worked the big bag to be ready for Illimani. By the end of April, he was in the best physical shape of his life. Mentally and emotionally, he was still struggling some, but physical demands of his regiment left him little time to dwell on his woes.

CHAPTER TWENTY
WHEN IS ENOUGH, ENOUGH?

Gabe had done yoga before while living in Colorado, specifically to help become a better climber and hiker, plus to prevent injury while in the mountains. Yoga compliments climbing because it helps not only with strength and flexibility, but also the mental aspect of being in the alpine. Many yoga and meditation-inspired breathing practices translate help climbers remain calm and rational during stressful or dangerous situations.

Mistakes on a mountain can be life threatening, and it's neither unusual nor surprising that many climbers panic when faced with unexpected missteps or accidents. Gabe knew this from experience as he had freaked out on a mountain more than once. He came to appreciate the mental benefits of the practice, and yoga became part of his daily life. He hadn't been practicing yoga regularly in Bolivia, but it was time to start again, to stabilize himself mentally for his final six months away from home.

What followed for Gabe was some yoga studio shopping since there were surprisingly several studios nearby to choose from. Eventually, he selected the studio two blocks from his apartment. It had no name. It appeared on Google Maps as *yoga,* lower case *y*. Gabe's kind of place.

Gabe reached out to the instructor, letting him know of his interest. The teacher pointed to a calendar of class schedules and suggested that he swing by for a class and check things out. So, on a garden-variety Tuesday evening in January, Gabe took his first yoga class in another country, in another language. He walked into the unassuming residential building where the studio was located; the instructor had rented the entire first floor. Walking through the kitchen, Gabe placed his personal belongings in a small adjacent room and stepped into the studio itself. You'd never think so from the outside, but it was a nice little studio able to accommodate about a dozen students. It was narrow with wood floors and maneki-nekos all over the room. The other students were all Bolivians.

Gabe asked the instructor if his limited understanding of Spanish would be a problem, and he said it wouldn't be. Since he knew Gabe was still learning the language, like any good teacher, the yogi kept the conversations strictly in Spanish. Uncomfortable of course, but important long-term. Busily trying to interpret his words, Gabe would always be a step behind both teacher and students in transitioning from pose to pose.

Everyone got situated, and Gabe's initial yoga class started off as expected. Breathing techniques and exercises, some warmup poses, nothing out of the ordinary. Child's pose, cat-cow, sun salutations, etc. After a few minutes, everyone got into the flow of the practice: downward dogs, warrior I and II, chair, and other common poses. Then, things got weird.

Gabe had learned that many yoga instructors take a few minor liberties in adding personal touches to their practices. For example, back in Colorado, his yoga instructor incorporated poses and techniques beneficial for rock climbing—minor differences here and there, but all seamlessly woven into the standard practices.

This individual Bolivian yoga instructor took his personal touches to an entirely different level. It was like the offspring of yoga and jazzercize. For people of a certain age, Jane Fonda's workout would come to mind from the yoga practiced that night. It started with activities like running in place, then everyone would get in line and run back and forth within the studio. Many times, they incorporated various ballet-style dance moves. They'd twirl, pirouette, stomp the floor with their feet, and do all kinds of aerobic movements. Even the music was different. It was neither calming nor New Age, but high-energy Latin sounds. It was like Gabe was a little cheerleader.

That first night, Gabe thought to himself, *Is this even yoga?*

But he went with it. *Why not? Try something different.* He followed all the other students and embraced this unique form. Sweat was pouring off everyone, both instructor and students. For close to an hour, everyone ran and jumped around excitedly.

Like with everything in Bolivia, Gabe was uncomfortable. But he attempted to keep an open mind.

One aspect of the class that he fully enjoyed was thirty full minutes of *savasana,* or corpse pose. It involved lying flat on the floor and letting go, and usually yoga teachers leave five or at most ten minutes for it at the end of class. A great way for Gabe to get into a calming, meditative state.

He had gone through meditative practices years before in an attempt to find his spirit animal, which surprised him as being a rabbit. But in this class, he was able to enter a mental state much more deeply. He wasn't sure if it was the fast-paced aerobic movements or the intense concentration needed to focus on the poses being described in Spanish, but as he sank into his mat, he was able to be present. Slowly, he became more aware of the impacts, the beauty, and ultimately the power of yoga and meditation, which he was to take with him off the mat.

• • •

By the end of January, Gabe was feeling better. He was still struggling financially and questioning his success or lack thereof, but he had stopped the downward spiral. It was then that he made another commitment to himself. By his birthday in late February, he would make the decision either to remain in Bolivia after his year was completed, or to move back to the US. He was giving himself four to six more weeks of good, honest work to make progress with the fundraising. It would be his fortieth birthday gift to himself. But his decision on whether to stay longer was probably made, subconsciously, well before that birthday. He just didn't recognize it at the time.

After Gabe's mom and aunt visited in October, and after the three weeks spent with his Uncle Steve and other family and friends over the Christmas holiday, there was almost no chance he could have stayed away for longer than a year. He knew that he missed everyone and everything from home. He also missed the consistent water supply, the scheduled trash collections, the healthcare system, the FDA.

Gabe weighed all the pros and cons of staying, just like he did before deciding to move to Bolivia in the first place. Pros of staying included doing important work, establishing more relationships, and finding more candidate project locations. The cons of being away from family and friends, sacrificing career growth, and possibly confronting his mental state. Not unimportant was also having to communicate in Spanish for the unforeseeable future. There were also the rhetorical and existential questions that he kept asking himself:

What are the personal thresholds and limits of doing social good?

How much should one sacrifice to help others?

How much more can I, personally, handle, so that I can continue to give to people in need?

When is enough, enough?

Without proper self-care, Gabe realized, he wasn't really able to help others. It's like the rule on the airplane; in case of emergency, put on your own oxygen mask before helping others.

• • •

By his fortieth birthday, Gabe decided to return to Colorado in June—just four months away. By this point, he was healthy enough to realize that he had achieved many goals. Two were to establish operations so Pidola could develop and launch projects from the US, and to find candidate communities for new project locations. Through his new relationship with the Ministry of Education, he had identified locations where Pidola's projects would be a great fit. The operational pieces had been established as well. There was the Bolivian-based entity, Accendo SRL, enabling Pidola to execute contracts, and Luis the power of attorney who could execute all of those contracts. In addition, there was now a legal team, a bank account, an accountant, a public relations person, project developers and installers, and a strong relationship with ABE, the Bolivian equivalent of NASA. After those tough eight months, Pidola had everything needed to move forward and operate from back in Colorado.

The last goal Gabe achieved? Starting to better understand how to dust himself off when life tossed him onto the ground, no matter how thick that dust may be. He recalled the thick layer that had coated him and the others when they arrived in Pampa Jasi all those months ago. All it took to rid himself of that was a shower. This other type of dust would take a lot more effort.

CHAPTER TWENTY-ONE
BLACK MARKET GASOLINE

The Ministry of Education wanted Gabe to visit a dozen or so schools near the town of Villa Tunari to confirm that these locations would align well with the resources that Pidola could provide. In less than a week, he was on a flight from La Paz back to Cochabamba and coordinating logistics to visit schools around Villa Tunari. This trip would be his first to the area of the Amazon River Basin.

Gabe was excited to visit some additional project locations. It was one of the main reasons for being in South America, after all. But he was also scared about staying in the hotel where only three months before he had imagined it could have been his last visit.

Is staying there smart?

Safe?

Should I even put myself into this situation?

He took the chance and reserved a room at the Gran Hotel Paloma. It was surprising—and a testament to some rest at home, tough physical training, yoga, and meditation—that he had been able to stabilize himself mentally in just a couple of months. His head was clear enough to take the trip and to see if he could possibly get another project completed and launched, maybe even before he left.

It also occurred to Gabe that it might be time to change his approach. Isolation had caused him misery. Maybe now it was time to concentrate not on surviving but, instead, on thriving at being alone. Salvation lies within, right?

So he leaned into it.

After arriving in Cochabamba, he took a cab to the hotel. He stopped in front of the hotel's front doors and took a deep breath. He scanned his mind, body, and heart to see how he was truly feeling, and for the briefest of moments—probably less than a second—he had a flicker of inner peace.

It was enough for him to know that that night, and for at least that short trip to Cochabamba, he was going to be okay. Maybe he'd be even more than okay.

• • •

Gabe hired a driver, Miguel, who picked him up from the hotel at five the next morning. The trip to the town of Villa Tunari would be between four and five hours. It would be an even longer day for Miguel, since overnight he drove the Toyota pickup all the way from La Paz. The total time behind the wheel for him would be more than twenty-four hours.

Making small talk—all Gabe could handle since his Spanish was still limited—he learned that Miguel lived in El Alto, which immediately set him at ease. Gabe had experience relating well to people from El Alto. That city borders La Paz and sits above it. In Gabe's mind, it compared to Philadelphia in that it was rough, gritty, raw. Parts of La Paz were some of the most affluent neighborhoods in all of Bolivia, and El Alto had none of that.

Miguel was a family man with two kids and was a supporter of one of the local soccer teams. He seemed very salt-of-the-earth.

Thank goodness the interpreter, Lidy, was also on the trip. She lived in Cochabamba, so it was easy to bring her along for this little adventure into the jungle. Ever since she had told her story about smuggling Bibles, Gabe had been a fan. She added another layer of comfort; not only did they have a good relationship, but also she had a good understanding of Pidola's goals and projects. They were going to some remote places, so being at ease with the Bolivians traveling with him would go a long way.

Before sunrise, they cruised through Cochabamba and up the mountains toward the province of Chapare. This road trip was unique because of the dramatic change in topography. Between Cochabamba and the top of the mountain pass down to Villa Tunari, the climate was dry and the land barren and brown. They climbed to the pass, then descended for the next three hours along winding roads into the lush green jungle that was the beginning of the Amazon River Basin. Both landscapes were very different from the high desert of La Paz. It was only two hundred miles, as the crow flies, between La Paz and Villa Tunari, but with an eleven-thousand-foot drop in elevation between the two cities. Desert versus jungle, just as Gabe would have imagined.

Culturally, there were vast differences between the two areas as well. The cultural variety within Bolivia, a country roughly the size of Alaska, was extraordinary. La Paz's Andean culture included traditional foods like chicken, quinoa, rice, and potatoes—and warm clothes. In the Amazon, fruits and fish were the dominant foods and the clothing was lighter. In both places, various indigenous languages were spoken, but not the same ones.

Focusing on this specific area made sense to Gabe because the federal government of Bolivia had recently mandated the development of ways to preserve and support indigenous groups' ways of life, and Pidola projects would be an aspect of that larger program; energy and the internet could help them digitize and preserve their languages. It was one of the benefits, in Gabe's humble opinion, of having Evo Morales as president—his genuine commitment to the dozens of indigenous groups throughout Bolivia.

So off they went, up and over the pass, and down the approximately eight-thousand-foot drop into the jungles of Eastern Bolivia. The drive was spectacular. They passed through valleys of lush green forests as inverted clouds and a pleasant mixed bag of showers and sunlight welcomed them. The group was in good spirits.

The roads, on the other hand, were less inspiring. The road from Cochabamba to Villa Tunari was one of the key supposed highways moving people and goods from place to place, but they use the term *highway* loosely. In Bolivia. This road frequently went down to barely one lane and there was construction underway for nearly the entire drive. Despite the difficult conditions, drivers had total disregard for traffic laws and driving etiquette, and it was a white-knuckle experience for Gabe. Bolivia was infamous for the number of highway deaths per capita, and Gabe constantly heard news stories about buses colliding head-on in the middle of the night, killing dozens of people. For Gabe, the road system was reminiscent of the American Wild West, yet he felt somewhat at ease thanks to Miguel's skillful and practiced driving.

• • •

They rolled into Villa Tunari mid-morning and took a break before visiting the various schools in the area: Santa Elena de Los Yuracares, San Mateo Bajo, and Villa Gral. Roman. Of the dozen or so schools close to Villa Tunari, all needed some level of upgrading and maintenance, but most were relatively close to the already established infrastructure around town. Servicing this area would be easier and feasible, but the need didn't seem to be as great as many other rural and isolated villages and towns of Bolivia; they were not the next Pampa Jasi. Then, in the late afternoon, they visited two last locations: La Mision and San Jose de la Angosta.

Gabe had been introduced to the directors of the schools in these towns by contacts at the Ministry of Education, and they in turn vouched for Gabe and his American-based company. They would welcome him.

Gabe had been in contact with the directors of each of these schools for close to a week. Even though they didn't have access to power or the internet or cell service, many of the adults had cell phones and could use them when they came into Villa Tunari.

From Villa Tunari northwest toward Isiboro National Park, Miguel drove for about an hour on sandy roads that twisted through a dense jungle. La Mision, which sat next to a river, was a small community of about a half dozen buildings, the largest being the schoolhouse. About a hundred children went to school in this community, with most of the families living in small huts and sheds in the jungle beyond the open grassy area that surrounded the buildings. Here Gabe learned that many of the very small villages throughout the forest had just been *civilized* within the last thirty to forty years. He heard stories that some villagers around La Mision still went unclothed and used stereotypical spears for hunting. That made Gabe even more appreciative of having both Miguel and Lidy with him. He was surely an unknown and maybe even an unwelcome visitor.

Meeting the director and some of the other teachers of La Mision was both a wonderful and eye-opening experience. Like so many villages all over the country, La Mision didn't have the resources to effectively teach their children in the modern digital world. Since La Mision had no electrical power, computers, or access to the internet, almost all children were on a vocational path, primarily woodworking, regardless of what their interests were. Without the resources Pidola could provide, the educators' hands were tied. They were at the mercy of the government to provide them with power, internet, and computer hardware. In Gabe's estimation, it could take twenty years before La Mision would be connected to a reliable power grid. Hence the need for Pidola's projects.

It was a great visit, and the school definitely qualified as a good candidate. Gabe spent time with the director and teachers, learning about how they could positively affect the entire community. At the end of the visit, Gabe even learned some basic Yuracare vocabulary; one of the languages dying and which the community of La Mision was trying to maintain and document for preservation. He was humbled knowing he could have been only one of very few Westerners to have ever heard this language.

• • •

With good feelings and spirits, Gabe, Lidy, and Miguel made their way to the next and last community for the day, the village of San Jose de la Angosta. As with the school director of La Mision, Gabe had been texting the director for days about the visit. All was confirmed. The group started farther down the sandy roads, deeper into the jungle. Soon, the road they were on was overgrown with trees, and almost too narrow for their small Toyota pickup.

When the rainy season started in this tropical area, many areas became unreachable due to swollen rivers, washed-out roads, or general bad weather. Fortunately, the dry season had begun, but the rivers were still running high. This didn't stop Miguel from driving right into the thirty-meter-wide river and fording four-plus feet of water to get across. The water was high enough that when Gabe reached out of the window of the truck, he could touch it. Miguel seemed at ease, so Gabe and Lidy took it all in stride, despite exchanging a few quizzical looks.

The next river, the last step before reaching San Jose de la Angosta, was impassable. It was only about fifty yards wide, but deep enough that no vehicle could traverse it. It was the literal end of the road. So, like the community members, the group took a small boat across to reach San Jose de la Angosta. Gabe was thinking the entire time, *How on earth are we going to get all our large solar and internet equipment across this river? Are there even boats to accommodate this type of equipment?*

At both La Mision and San Jose de la Angosta, Gabe and Lidy walked around the community upon arrival. Since Gabe had been in contact with both schools' directors, he anticipated that they—or a teacher, or *someone*—would see the group and come up to introduce themselves. That's exactly what occurred in La Mision; they met a teacher as Gabe was taking pictures of the various buildings in the community for his reports. They did the same in San Jose de la Angosta. Lidy and Gabe meandered through and past the various buildings, taking pictures and making themselves at home.

What Gabe didn't realize was that the school director wasn't physically *in* San Jose de la Angosta, and that he hadn't mentioned to anyone within the community that they were visiting. So they were caught off guard when a group of five men approached them, angrily asking who they were and wanting to know what they were doing there. Gabe was taken aback by this heated reception, figuring that the men were wary of strangers, especially Anglo ones. And when he looked at Lidy's face he knew something was wrong. Her initial explanation hadn't calmed the locals' agitation. It would be a good five to ten minutes of intense discussion about why they were there and that they had been invited by the director before things cooled down. Gabe wondered what the outcome would have been if Lidy hadn't been there to act as diplomatic liaison. Seeing a worried expression on the face of a woman who had once been in an Iranian jail was unsettling. Gabe had not been overly fearful of injury since arriving in Bolivia, other than on those Illi training treks through La Paz encountering wild dogs and unsavory characters.

It was getting late in the day and the three visitors still had to ford a river, get back to Villa Tunari, and drive back through the mountains to Cochabamba—all best done before nightfall. They would cross the river in the daylight, but the mountain driving would take place in the pitch dark. Again, Gabe was glad Miguel would be at the wheel.

River crossing and sandy roads behind them, Miguel eventually pulled onto a paved thoroughfare that would lead back to Villa Tunari.

The closer to town, the better. Gabe took a moment to reflect on the successful day of site visits. Even though they had another hour back to Villa Tunari, and then another four to five hours to Cochabamba, he was in good spirits.

Then, Miguel said, *"Nos estamos quedando sin gasolina."* Lidy and Gabe looked at one another, and concern washed over both of them. Gabe hadn't thought of it since they left Cochabamba, but Miguel hadn't stopped for gas since early that morning. Now, they were running on fumes.

What do we do if we run out of gas?

How far are we from the closest gas station?

How dangerous of a situation are we in?

Gabe was further surprised that his question about the nearest gas station wasn't even relevant. A local regulation, at least in and around Villa Tunari, was that all gas stations were required by law to close at sunset, which reduced the incidence of fuel theft. Even if they made it back to Villa Tunari, no gas stations would be open.

Gabe had slept in his truck several times back in Colorado, so he guessed he could sleep in a truck in Bolivia, too.

Just as on the river, Miguel seemed very much at ease in this situation, shrugging off the misstep as commonplace. Miguel knew that in this part of Bolivia anyone needing gas after dark just hits the market—the black market. There was an actual black market on a street in Villa Tunari, complete with dozens of vendors selling various items: clothes, tools, auto parts, cleaning supplies, etc., like a basic American flea market. They would just need to find one of the vendors that had a fifty-gallon drum of gas in the back of their store.

Miguel asked a guy selling car parts if he had gas, and they rolled out a few gallons. Miguel fueled the truck at three times the cost of the normal price—hardly a surprise. Still, another crisis had been averted and they had enough fuel to get them back to Cochabamba.

After Villa Tunari, Miguel started up the mountain, complete with valleys and switchbacks that they'd traversed just a little more than twelve hours earlier. Only this time, going up, it was now raining and dark. Really dark, especially since there were no streetlights. There was barely a road at some points. Gabe was exhausted, just too tired to dwell on the perils of the trip or worry about those to come. He felt oddly at peace.

Lidy was sleeping in the back and Gabe was daydreaming in the passenger seat. For whatever reason, he looked over at Miguel, and noticed that he wasn't keeping his eyes open. Gabe remembered that Miguel had been up for well over twenty-four hours. The man must have been more exhausted than either Gabe or Lidy. Knowing how dangerous this driving could be, Gabe asked Miguel in his broken Spanish, "Are you okay? Do you want me to drive?"

What had he just said? He couldn't believe what had come out of his mouth.

Drive?

Me?

In this?

Am I insane?

Driving on those roads was total chaos even without the rain. And without streetlights. Plus they were sharing the road with huge eighteen-wheelers.

To Gabe's utter disbelief, Miguel said, "*Si, puedes conducir.*" Yes, you can drive.

Uh-oh.

It appeared that Gabe wasn't going to die by taking a leap out of the hotel in Cochabamba. *No, my final resting place would be somewhere on the road between Villa Tunari and Cochabamba.* Miguel pulled over and they switched driver and passenger; Lidy didn't even stir. *Thank goodness I know how to drive stick-shift.*

Off they went. Initially, Gabe nestled in behind one of the large semitrucks and thought that if he could just follow him back to Cochabamba, him being a "lead blocker," he'd be just fine. But going five miles per hour the entire time was unrealistic; it would take another twelve hours to get back at that rate. He figured, *I've driven in Australia,*

Africa, Europe, and of course home in North America. He sucked in his gut and told himself, *Buck up man. It's time to drive properly in South America, too.*

Coming up on short straightaways, Gabe found the courage to pass that semitruck in front and then a second and a third. Some crazy Bolivians were also passing him, but he was making decent progress. He couldn't see much of anything due to the rain, fog, and pitch-black night, but he was driving, nonetheless. Weaving in and out of traffic, dodging cars coming down the mountain, he felt that he had been initiated into a new, practically extra-terrestrial club—drivers of the Amazon River Basin.

Even though he was exhausted, Gabe had enough focus and energy to get them up and over the pass, which eventually would lead down into Cochabamba. If nothing else, nerves kept him alert.

Meanwhile, Miguel napped for a couple hours. They switched seats again at a toll on the road to Cochabamba. Switching out was a smart move. Gabe's day had been exciting enough, and he would have preferred not to get thrown into a Bolivian jail for not having his driver's license.

Project scouting among complete strangers, river fording, being threatened by unfriendly Bolivians, purchasing black-market gasoline, and driving for the first time in South America. It was a long day, a successful day, one of the best days Gabe had that year.

CHAPTER TWENTY-TWO
19,987

The rest of February and through March were relatively quiet from a work standpoint, so Gabe returned to his training for Illimani. It was also time for Gabe to venture out a little; it had been a while since he went exploring. It was time to finally head to the amateur wrestling matches up in El Alto.

During one of his previous trips to La Paz, Gabe had heard of these amateur wrestling matches up in El Alto. These matches also came up when researching things to do in La Paz, so it had piqued Gabe's interest for the last few years. It was time to make the short trip up to El Elto and witness the Cholitas Wrestling Show.

A Cholita can be defined as a woman who self-identifies themselves as an indigenous person from primarily Andean culture—Aymaran, Quechuan, etc. In typical style, these women are usually shorter, with bowler hats, a fitted corset, and a bright-colored skirt. Cholitas can be found everywhere in La Paz, but seeing them participate in wrestling matches would surely be a novelty. There was also a well-known group of Cholitas that climbed the various high-peaks throughout Bolivia—the Climbing Cholitas. Gabe had heard that they are some of the strongest climbers anywhere in South America.

So, up to El Alto Gabe went. He found the address and location of the matches, which could be loosely equated to something like an average high school gymnasium. There wasn't much in terms of seating; maybe five hundred people could buy a ticket for the show. A ticket, and a bag of popcorn.

People filed in and the makeshift arena slowly filled. Gabe thought it was nice that the organizers of the event also provided a snack, which he picked at slowly. He didn't notice that everyone else around him also had a bag of popcorn but weren't actually eating theirs. So, after a few of the matches started, he then realized why popcorn was provided as part of the ticket.

The crowd not only watched the matches, but they were also active participants! The popcorn was to be used to throw at the villainous Cholitas when they won a match. Popcorn eventually ended up everywhere throughout the gymnasium.

• • •

Gabe was getting ready for the Teleferico ride in Zona Sur after a long conversation with his lawyers about general legal requirements needed for the company. He stepped out of the four-story building and looked up the valley toward his neighborhood of Sopocachi. It had been nice weather as he'd come down the valley just a couple hours before, but he was now looking at looming dark clouds to the northwest, clouds with the type of color that make anyone want to immediately take shelter.

He stepped onto the gondola and temporarily put the possibility of bad weather out of his mind. The gentle swaying as usual put him into a good—or at least better—mood, and his mind wandered toward other things, like heading back to the US in just a couple of months. That thought had been all encompassing recently, barely allowing other thoughts to come to mind.

The Teleferico had one stop between Zona Sur and where Gabe lived in Sopocachi, a line change from green to yellow. As he entered the changeover station of Chuqui Apu, the ominous clouds were overhead. What had been a peaceful fall day in Bolivia turned threatening. Frustrated, Gabe realized he was going to get soaked on the walk home. It never occurred to him that the entire cable car system would be shut down. In the ten months since Gabe moved to the city, he had never heard, not one time, of the gondolas being stopped for any reason. In a city and country that seems to always have infrastructure problems and issues, the Teleferico was the one thing someone could rely on. Like clockwork.

Gabe stepped off the green line and toward the turnstiles for the yellow line. It was late in the day, so there were more people using the system—the start of rush hour commuting. As he waited his turn to flash his Teleferico card, the blackened clouds opened up and the rains began. First it was just typical sprinkles, then a steadier rain, then a torrential downpour. It was the type of downpour that immediately made him think that something was going to flood. A street, buildings, the river that ran through the city. Something. On any given day, Gabe could see up the valley wall to the final Teleferico station on the yellow line where La Paz ended, and El Alto began. The rain now hid that station—and every other station in between—from view.

Then the unthinkable happened. The Teleferico stopped. Gabe couldn't believe it. It wasn't that windy, so maybe it was just that the rain was coming down so hard the system had to be paused for passenger safety. It was a relief to Gabe to think that the operators of the Teleferico system were conscious of passenger safety and did have those checks and balances in place. Good. He just needed to wait until the storm passed and then off he would go up into Sopocachi.

The cabled gondolas were only stopped for a handful of minutes; the storm passed quickly. The cabins started to move again, and people started flowing in and out. Back to normal. Gabe got into his yellow gondola with seven other passengers, which started up the valley wall. The pitch-black clouds had now moved over the city, down the valley and toward the good folks of Cochabamba. It was still sprinkling as Gabe's cabin moved over the southern part of Sopocachi and toward his station.

Gabe stepped out of the Teleferico station and started walking the five blocks back home. In the distance came police or ambulance sirens, but again, he felt unphased. Anyone who lives in a big city worldwide hears sirens almost constantly; they just become background noise. Gabe pushed them aside and the walk back to his apartment was uneventful.

When Gabe reached his apartment and started to settle in, he opened the windows to let in some post-storm fresh air. The sirens still blared but were louder and closer than before. Close enough to take notice. After a few more minutes of settling in, more sirens. Louder. Closer. This wasn't your typical traffic stop or call or an ambulance. Something significant was happening close to Gabe's apartment. He turned on the TV, which was a rarity since all the stations were in Spanish and TV wasn't really a part of his day-to-day lifestyle.

Gabe flipped around to find a news station. Lo and behold, he found a channel with a flash story. There was a reporter who seemed to be right near the Chuqui Apu station, the same station that Gabe passed through about thirty minutes before. The reporter's voice was animated, and Gabe sensed something was seriously wrong.

Behind the reporter was a massive mudslide. Not the kind where just a few rocks and debris crossed a road. This mudslide had taken out dozens and dozens of houses that had long been a part of the neighborhood of Sopocachi. Gabe looked more closely. Some of them were actually close to his apartment building. The sirens were only about ten blocks away.

The mudslide was just under the yellow Teleferico line and must have happened right after Gabe went over the area after the storm. Much of the chaos and craziness that Gabe would hear about while living in Bolivia always seemed like a distant event. This one was happening right around the corner.

Gabe would later learn that that part of the Sopocachi neighborhood was built on an old trash dump. The ground was less than stable and less than ideal for development. The news in the coming days would state that sixty-six homes were destroyed, and hundreds of people left homeless. Thankfully, no one was killed.

• • •

Illi now was Gabe's focal point. Day after day, week after week, he worked on aspects of the upcoming climb. The physical prep continued both in the street and in the gym, and as the end of April approached, logistics needed to be organized.

On he and his friend's previous attempt on Illimani many years prior, Gabe had used a guide from a service out of La Paz. A local organization that not only had offices close to Gabe's apartment, but also one of the less-expensive services that he could find. Guide and cook were available for pennies on the dollar, which was critical since Gabe was still on a shoestring budget. It was a decent service, definitely good enough to patronize a second time. If nothing else, they cooked good food—high in calories and well-prepared.

Gabe was assigned two men to join him—mountain guide Carlos and Sergio, a cook.

April 30 was to be the start date, and it arrived quickly. Gabe met his individual guide, Carlos, at their offices and ran through the gear checklist: tent, sleeping bag, sleeping mat, pillow, base layers, mid-layers, shells, multiple pairs of socks and underwear, puffy gloves, oh-shit-mitts, beanie, a second beanie, a third beanie, glacier sunglasses, goggles, regular sunglasses, full-brimmed hat, hiking boots, hiking poles, crampon-compatible boots, gaiters, crampons, ice ax, mountaineering ax, helmet, alpine rope, Garmin GPS device, slings, cordelette, harness, prusiks, ice screws, a half-dozen carabiners, sunscreen, toiletries, medications, food, cooking stove and fuel, utensils, fire starter, Nalgene water bottles. Forty pounds of gear in all, which was his personal limit of weight to carry.

With the gear check completed, the three men loaded up yet another Toyota 4Runner and started southeast for a four- to five-hour drive to Pinaya, a small town at the base of Illi and the launching point for the standard route up the mountain. As they made their way, Gabe was feeling good, both physically and mentally. Four months of training at the high altitude of La Paz was a great conditioning and altitude acclimatization. He had also met all his work deadlines and wrapped up everything that needed to be done for Pidola. All he had to focus on was the task at hand. Plus, the weather window was looking great, so they had a good chance for a summit attempt. It was going to be four days on the mountain. Gabe would be out of cell phone reception; he'd have no way to check emails or take any calls. The next four days were going to be just for him. Life became simple.

They stopped at a small village about halfway between La Paz and Pinaya, for a break to grab their last meal underroof before having all subsequent meals outdoors. The small town was like the dozens of others he had visited, with a small square, dirt roads, and a dozen or so small buildings. Gabe, Carlos, and Sergio popped into the only restaurant in town for lunch. Knowing that he'd be burning thousands of calories over the next few days, Gabe ate as much as he could, and continued to hydrate in preparation for the massive amounts of sweating ahead. Because he had been so focused on getting himself physically ready for the climb, he was taken aback when he looked across the restaurant and saw Carlos slugging beers. Gabe was in possibly the best shape of his life yet wouldn't even think about touching alcohol right before a climb. And here was this short, stocky Bolivian guide hammering drinks and not worried whatsoever about his physical preparedness. *You get what you pay for*, Gabe thought to himself.

Back in the vehicle, Gabe full of food, Carlos half drunk, they drove the next couple of hours to Pinaya. The drive, like the one from Torotoro to Pampa Jasi, was both terrifying and beautiful. The roads were narrow and made with dirt and stone, the valley walls thousands of vertical feet high. Up and down, around blind turns, over bridges with streams bursting from glacial runoff. Everything on the way to Illimani was just big. It was harrowing at times passing other cars or pedestrians, but also inspiring.

As they came into Pinaya, Gabe was taken (aback?) by the contrasts ahead. The small valley leading up onto Illimani was very green, with trees and smaller vegetation benefiting from the water melting off the glacier. So, there's an opportunity for more people to live in this small valley; probably a few hundred people with a few dozen two- and three-room homes. Carlos was born and still maintained a house in the village, which was why he had been able to climb the mountain close to three hundred times. There wasn't much to Pinaya in terms of infrastructure or creature comforts, but what it lacked in those areas, it made up for in natural beauty.

Pulling in after a three-hour drive, they unloaded gear onto the town's soccer field. Given that it was just going to be Carlos, Gabe, and Sergio, they had an inordinate amount of stuff. Gabe felt embarrassed that the food they'd packed for just four days would have fed a family in Pinaya for a month. The longer they hung out, the more he would have had to feel ashamed, so he told Carlos he was ready, and they started right away up to the first campsite, about two hours off.

• • •

Sergio and Carlos took much of the gear and went ahead, while Gabe slowly followed with his pack, through town and then up the base of the mountain. At around fourteen thousand feet, things become magical. As Gabe well knew, on almost any big peak, a climber reaches a certain altitude where things just, well, stop existing—no trees, grass, bushes, or weeds. Without that vegetation there were fewer animals.

Mountainscapes at high altitudes could feel barren and cold, like being on Mars. Alpine environments were among Gabe's favorite places anywhere in the world. When he stepped into this landscape where there's little life, it was clear he was not supposed to be there. He was sustained by only what he could carry, what was on his back. Being at high altitude provided him a raw, visceral experience.

Camp One was about three thousand vertical feet below where the glacier starts on Illimani. It was a relatively comfortable campsite, not yet high enough to really feel the effects of altitude, and there's a small patch of grass that was flatter than Gabe's Bolivian bed. That was where the group had pitched the tents. The sun was setting behind them, and Sergio had already prepared dinner. Since Gabe had self-guided many trips in Colorado and on Washington State's Mount Rainier, he knew that, so far, this climb was the classic walk in the park.

As they settled in and got ready for a meal of chicken, rice, and bread, the stars started to pop. Camp One was on the other side of Illimani from La Paz, so to the northwest there was very little light pollution and to the southeast the nearest large city was nine thousand miles away. The sky was as clear as one can imagine. Gabe would have a few similar nights before leaving Bolivia, looking at the stars of the Southern Hemisphere, and reflecting on how everyone he cared about was looking at an entirely different sky. That reminded him of how alone he was, how easy it was for distance to creep in between us and even our closest loved ones. Gabe was glad he'd made the decision to move back to the States in late June.

Most people don't sleep well at altitude, and Gabe was no exception, especially since he had a condition similar to sleep apnea. When at higher altitudes, mainly above twelve thousand feet, his breathing patterns would get disrupted, and he would wake up in the middle of the night gasping for air. It was nothing he ever concerned himself with since it was harmless—more of an annoyance. People sleeping next to him, however, almost always thought he was in serious trouble. He would get a chuckle out of it; his team never did.

Gabe knew his nights on the trip would be long and restless, and the first night was no exception. After a handful of hours' sleep, he woke up the next morning for breakfast, after which they started on the next leg of the climb. The higher he and Carlos went, the smaller he felt. Below Illimani's glacier, everything they passed was brown and rocky. The blue skies, the gleaming white glacier, and the brown and reds of the rock made for a gorgeous hike. Progressing slowly, they eventually scrambled their way to the camp called *Nido de Condores*, the Condor's Nest. It was just a small patch of open area on one of the ribs of Illimani, and naturally protected since it sits slightly above the ice and snow surrounding it—a good thing since it is in serious avalanche terrain. Every fifteen minutes or so, Gabe would hear calving—the breaking off ice from the glacier. The ice would fall into the valleys below, which was unnerving. Some of the falls were only a few hundred yards from the tents. They were protected, but the loud crashes still scared the hell out of him.

The Condor's Nest was the high camp where they would spend their last night before attempting the summit the next morning. Gabe felt good. On his previous attempt years before, his AMS began at Condor's Nest. His head was splitting the night before they were to push for the summit, a feeling like his brain was melting. This time around, he was relieved that his head was still clear. He was going to at least attempt the summit.

There was a beautiful sunset that night, and they were now high enough to see Sajama. From the Condor's Nest, they could also see Lake Titicaca. As the sun started to sink below the horizon, Gabe settled in to grab at least an hour or two of sleep. They were having an alpine start, which meant they were going to wake up at midnight for a climb in the dark, and summit around sunrise. Most climbers do this just so they can get back to camp during daylight and avoid being exposed to the elements for too long.

Midnight came. Gabe's head was still feeling pretty good, so they strapped their crampons on, slipped their legs into their harnesses, and grabbed their mountaineering axes for the push onto the glaciated part of the hike. Gabe rarely felt more comfortable than when he had crampons on his feet and an ice ax in his hand. There was something about climbing and traveling on the snow that just felt right to him, like how other people feel when rock climbing, surfing, or skydiving. He was a duck in water on the snow, and it felt natural to be on it again.

It was now just Carlos and Gabe. Since Carlos had been to this peak so many times, he knew the route and where to go on the glacier, even in the dark. It was a moonless night and Gabe's headlamp only lit the area immediately in front of him; everywhere else was pitch black. They had all the gear on and most of their clothing, too, since it was close to zero degrees when they started. But there was no wind, so they were comfortable and warm enough moving along at a steady pace.

After about an hour of climbing, they turned right to start up the last two thousand feet toward the summit. They were traversing just below a ridge about two hundred and fifty feet above them. Even though it was dark, they could slightly make out the snow and ridge now to their left when Gabe occasionally turned off his headlamp to check out the stars, and for the briefest of moments, he thought he saw a flash of light. They were at nineteen thousand eight hundred feet at this point, so he chalked it up to his mind not being 100 percent clear. Another zebra moment. Then, another flash of light. He looked around and above, but it was clear skies.

What the hell am I seeing?

"Did you see that light?" he asked Carlos.

"*Si, claro.*" It was lightning.

Gabe hadn't put two and two together. On the eastern slope of Illimani, there was a dramatic drop in elevation. Not all the way down to the jungle like in Villa Tunari, but enough to be in a vastly different climate zone. What they were seeing above the ridgeline was the lightning from a thunderstorm below them. It was now negative five degrees, no wind, and clear skies. The lightning lit up the area all around them for just those briefest of moments, and it was remarkable.

Knowing that they weren't in any danger, they stopped for a quick bite to eat and were about to start on their way for the final push. But, on this attempt, Gabe would ultimately not make the summit. After another hour of slow progress, both he and Carlos decided to turn back. Pure exhaustion had hit, and they wanted to make sure that Gabe had enough energy for the return trip. Gabe thought about a quote from the great high-altitude American mountaineer Ed Veisures. "*Up is optional, down is mandatory.*"

Gabe had turned around on many summits for safety or health reasons, and he knew this attempt on Illimani was over. They had climbed just thirteen feet shy of twenty thousand feet and were just over a thousand feet short of summit. Despite coming up short, Gabe was happy with his new personal best in altitude. Plus, the mountain wasn't going anywhere. He was utterly exhausted; one more step upward wasn't going to happen. And that was just fine.

His inner voice was silent. Instead, the narrative inside him was that he'd done well. He thought of what American writer and philosopher Robert Pirsig had said. "*It's the sides of the mountain that sustains things, not the top. Here's where things grow.*"

• • •

Gabe made it back to Pinaya later that day—a seemingly endless day. Gabe had heard of amazing stories where climbers would spend twelve, fourteen, or even twenty-plus hours in the death zone above twenty-six thousand feet in altitude and then, after coming down, would sleep for as much as twenty-four-plus hours. He found those stories incredible—that people could exert so much energy that their bodies just shut down completely when back in a safe place.

After three days on Illimani, Gabe slept for fourteen straight hours at his guide's house in Pinaya. After a shower and a full meal, pure exhaustion overcame him. Before he had fallen asleep, he reflected a bit not only about his time on Illimani, but also on surviving that mad drive from Villa Tunari. Since reaching his worst in December, he'd had some unique experiences. He took a moment of appreciation and gratitude for the last four months of his life, and then the lights out.

CHAPTER TWENTY-THREE
BIRDING

Gabe was excited for his brother, Larry, to visit in May. He knew the opportunities for growth that come with exploring new places and getting out of one's comfort zone. Gabe had lived, worked, studied, and spent time in more than forty countries on six continents, well-known places like London, Athens, Tokyo, Sydney, and Cape Town, and lesser-known places like Qomolangma, Orizaba, Ngorongoro, Rotorua, and Masada. These places made him who he was. When his head was clear, the blessings of all his travels were at the front of his mind.

Gabe was also excited for the opportunity to give Larry the experience of this beautiful and sometimes chaotic country, as he'd felt with his mom and aunt six months earlier. Even if he'd accomplished nothing else while living in South America, he could still be proud of having offered his family these experiences. A refreshing shift of perspective.

Over the Christmas holiday, lots of friends and family had told Gabe they would like to visit, but he knew they wouldn't. Over Christmas dinner, Larry had said, "I'm really coming to visit. Honest! I swear. I'll book the ticket." Gabe had his doubts. But when Larry booked his flights to La Paz in February, Gabe was impressed. Gabe often felt a little like an ambassador for the US when he was visiting some remote village. Now, he also felt a little like an ambassador for Bolivia.

• • •

Larry was a birder. He kept checklists of those birds he'd seen, and he had a list of those he hoped to see while in Bolivia. Gabe? He knew what a pigeon looked like. He had seen ducks and some geese. Even a robin here and there. That was pretty much the extent of his ornithology.

But Larry and Gabe did share one characteristic: they were both planners, and by spring they had their trip mapped out with precision. La Paz, Rurrenabaque and adjacent Madidi National Park, Tiwanaku, and finally Sajama National Park. For ten days, they were going to experience almost all of the ecosystems in Bolivia, as well as different cultures with their different types of food. They would also see a ton of birds; Larry informed him that the Bolivian jungle has one of the most diverse and highest concentrations of birds anywhere in the world.

The trip was also a chance for Gabe to get to know his brother better. Gabe was the youngest of three boys and two girls, and seven years separated him from the sibling closest to him in age. Larry was nineteen years older than Gabe. When Gabe was five, Larry was getting married, and when Gabe was a teenager, Larry was welcoming Gabe's niece into the world. They were never in the same life stage, so he believed they didn't have much in common. The ten days traveling together would not only be Larry's once-in-a-lifetime opportunity to see Bolivia, but also Gabe's chance to become closer to his brother.

When Larry arrived at the Bolivian airport, even though Gabe was in a much better headspace, he felt the same way he had when greeting his mom and aunt; he would set aside all his life's issues while spending time together. Even if it was just for a few days, problems could wait. This trip was for Larry.

The two brothers initially caught up on general family news, work, weather, and sports. Gabe knew that each member of his family was capable of deep discussions, but most of their conversations were breezy. Then, they did the standard tourist activities in and around La Paz that by now Gabe had mastered: the cable cars, the Witches Market, Calle Jaen. He knew La Paz so well after eleven months that he was also able to introduce Larry to the less touristy areas. The first night, they both gravitated toward an Argentinian restaurant, not a Bolivian one, which made them both chuckle. Larry didn't even have time to acclimatize, since the next day they were back at the airport, catching an hour's long flight northeast to Rurrenabaque called "Rurre" for short.

Rurre was similar to Villa Tunari in size, culture, topography, and climate. Both places were part of Amazonian culture. The Rurre's airport was by far the smallest airport Gabe had ever been to. The runway is so short that only planes carrying a dozen or so passengers could land. Taxiing only took a few moments. When the door opened, they immediately got slammed with heat and humidity. Larry also immediately started spotting birds, even before he left the airport: magpies, tanagers, and yellow-headed caracaras. Larry was a pig in mud. "Look! Did you see that bird? I can't believe we just saw a crazed hoatzin . . . unbelievable."

Gabe nodded.

Their guide, Raul, picked them up outside of the small, dilapidated terminal. A local, Raul had a wealth of knowledge about birds—colors and behaviors of the different genders, how to identify by their songs and calls, migration patterns, and more, plus locations where Larry could spot some of the more popular species. He was like a walking, talking Audubon mobile app. During the three-hour drive from the Rurre airport to Madidi National Park, Larry and Raul talked continually about Bolivian birds. The group stopped periodically along the way so Larry could take pictures. Clearly, the three of them were going to spend four days in Madidi looking at birds. Remembering this trip was primarily for Larry and not himself, Gabe played along and pretended to be interested, but inside my head ran the refrain, *Oy vey, what have I gotten myself into?*

The adventure entailed two hours via paved road, then a turn onto a dirt road, and up into the jungle for an hour. Gabe had seen some pretty sketchy roads during his time in Bolivia, but this road could be defined as beyond sketchy, possibly the new gold standard of crappy roads. The dirt-and-rock road had deteriorated so badly on the slope down toward a steep, large valley that any further loss of road would send the car into the forest. It was the only time Gabe asked a driver to pull to a stop so he could get out to walk certain stretches. Larry, who didn't feel the same dread, followed his younger brother's lead nonetheless. When roads literally ended you know you were deep in some remote place—in this case, the jungle.

Madidi National Park was a protected area of Bolivia, mainly from the logging, mining, and other heavy commercial activities that historically have destroyed the surrounding ecosystem. The park was lush, green, dense, hot, and humid. By taking a few steps off the trail, you could easily get lost.

They drove up and over a ridgeline and near the top gathered their belongings and walked about five minutes to the main lodge of the resort where they were staying. For the next three nights, they were very much unplugged. Gabe didn't even bring his laptop, since he knew that there would be no cell service, no WiFi, and not too much to speak of in terms of electricity. They were officially off the grid.

The lodge was a bare-bones operation. It had one main wooden building that acted as a kitchen and dining area with a nice wrap-around porch, and a half dozen or so smaller buildings where one or two people could rest their heads and keep their stuff. It was perfect for Gabe and Larry's needs, and for seeing birds. A two-story watchtower adjacent to the main building had just been constructed for birders. Gabe didn't know how much planning had been involved to erect the watchtower, nor did he have any engineering skills himself. What he did understand was that four vertical poles supporting a wooden platform wouldn't provide much stability. No support beams, no cross-sections. Being that Gabe and his brother were blood, however, and that neither of them were ever accused of being too smart, they made their way up the wobbly platform multiple times during the stay. Gabe doubted that the platform would survive too much longer after their trip.

The first two days were slow for Gabe, but he continued to tag along with Larry and Raul, observing birds, insects, monkeys, which he enjoyed, and various reptiles. As much as he was in his element on Illimani's glacier, he was totally outside it while in the jungle. One day, they saw trogans, tanagers, dacnis, and screaming pihas.

"Did you see that black-fronted nunbird?" Larry screamed with excitement, his face alive with joy.

"Yes, Larry, I saw it," Gabe answered while taking video of the leafcutter ants on the ground around them. Larry's excitement didn't wane, and Gabe's didn't spike. However, at some point on the third day, something strange happened. Gabe started to feel and act differently. He started looking for birds.

"Wait, is that a new one? Have we seen that one yet? What about that one there on the limb of that tree? There! How can you not see it?"

Gabe was suddenly interested in finding species that they hadn't seen. It was a challenge, and even fun. A strong-billed woodcreeper, a red-necked woodpecker, and a gray-breasted sabrewing. They were picking them out left and right.

What had gotten into him? Had he become a birder? Maybe not to the extent of Larry and Raul, but later he would later acquire a *Birds of Colorado* book which he continued to keep on his coffee table even after moving back to Philadelphia.

However, a larger transformation also happened at Madidi. During the day, they'd be out cataloging birds. But in the evening, Larry and

Gabe shared the same little two-bed bungalow near the main lodge. It was then that they really got to know one another better, and they connected like never before. They talked about work, their family, Larry's thoughts about retirement, Gabe's search for a purpose. They learned that they had some of the same concerns and fears and a host of similarities. Of course, staying within the style of their family, Gabe never fully shared the truth of the emotional and psychological stresses he was going through in Bolivia, but he knew that his support staff had just grown a bit bigger. He would never again be as isolated as he had been just a few months before. It reaffirmed that he did have a strong family behind him to lean into. It took going deep into the Bolivian jungle to better realize it.

In the end, Larry and Gabe identified more than one hundred species of birds and took thousands of pictures. Well, Larry did; Gabe took very few photos. Birds that were common, birds that they'd never see again. And after those four days, Gabe came to appreciate not only the skill and hobby of birdwatching, but also the joys of being with his brother. And Larry was glad that he'd opened up Gabe's world to a completely different activity. They had forged a deeper connection. Gabe began to wonder if maybe Larry's visit would benefit Gabe even more than it had Larry. So much for being the jaded world traveler of the two.

• • •

After Madidi, Larry and Gabe made their way back over the sketchy roads to Rurre for their flight to La Paz. Gabe was thankful that Larry enjoyed the time in the jungle, but he was relieved to leave the hot, humid climate and get back to the high desert of the Altiplano. There were way too many bugs in the jungle. Also, he would finally be getting to Sajama. Of course, they wouldn't be climbing Sajama, but something had drawn Gabe to this specific part of Bolivia, something innate that was hard to describe. After all the research, all the planning, and all the photos he had seen, he was more than ready to check this place out.

From La Paz, another driver in another 4Runner picked the two up to head to the national park. After climbing up and through El Alto, they stopped in Patacamaya for a quick lunch of dried, shredded llama meat called *Charque de Llama*. It surprised them both by being fabulous. They then drove straight for Sajama. The extinct volcano in the distance loomed larger mile after mile. Given that the area between La Paz and Sajama was primarily a high, flat plain, it at first seemed to just pop up out of nowhere. With the consistent blue skies behind her, Sajama was dramatic the entire drive in.

Then, suddenly, the guide made an unexpected turn. Gabe thought they were taking a break, but they entered the town of Curahuara de Carangas. It was the Pinaya of the high plains; no paved roads, no real infrastructure. A restaurant, maybe. A center square for sure, but not much else around it. Some one- or two-story buildings, some homes, few people. It was almost a ghost town, but they could tell some people still lived in the area since there were still stray dogs barking and roaming around.

The guide took Larry and Gabe to a building that looked like a church, but neither of them was sure. "What are we doing here?" they asked each other simultaneously.

At the building entrance, a petite older Andean woman asked them for a few Bolivianos as admission to enter the building. Gabe thought that was strange since he had no idea what the site was. He wondered if she was just asking for change. But since it was the equivalent of twenty-five US cents, he paid it.

As they walked through the doors, Gabe realized why the guide brought them to this small, quiet building in Western Bolivia. The walls and ceiling were an endless mosaic of Christian history. This little church was a world treasure, the Sistine Chapel of South America. *La Iglesia de Curahuara de Carangas*, or simply the church of Curahuara de Carangas, was and still is one of the best kept secrets Gabe had ever seen. He immediately loved it.

Built in 1608, the church was in some disrepair, but the dry and cool climate seemed to have preserved the artwork over the centuries. The colors were still brilliant, the detail meticulous. The images and stories were of both South American and European cultures and influences. Gabe had been fortunate to see many astonishing pieces of architecture, murals, paintings, and sculptures through all his travels. However, this little church captivated him to the point at which he forgot they were only an hour from the little hotel they'd be staying in on the far side of Sajama.

As the guide strode back to the 4Runner, Gabe remembered they were about to circumnavigate the peak.

In the national park there, the mountain stood alone. The entire top two-thirds of the peak resembled a coned ice cube, albeit twenty-one thousand feet tall. She was both imposing and sexy, and Gabe was finally at her base. He briefly wished this could have been a climbing expedition, but that would have to wait for another time.

All around Sajama and outside the park were other smaller volcanoes, mainly on the Chilean side of the border. Volcanoes with small plumes of smoke jetting from their sides. Peaks named *Parinacota, Acotango,* and *Patilla Pata.* The landscape was similar to all parts of the northern and western fringes of the Andes, and one of the driest areas in the world, if not the dryest. Some areas near Sajama and into the Atacama Desert in Chile haven't seen rain in four hundred years, which explained the barren landscape. Just like on the other side of Illimani, it was Martianesque. Very few bushes and small *Queñoa De Altura* trees grew sporadically.

The hotel where Larry and Gabe were staying was fifteen thousand feet above sea level, so there wasn't much of anything to be seen, plant or animal, which was vastly different from the abundance of life in Madidi. Gabe thoroughly enjoyed every second of it. Even though Larry started with the same mindset that Gabe had in Madidi, mainly going along for the ride, he was impressed, too.

A few places Gabe had visited have a certain magic. It's something, a feeling, which made these places special. Gabe wasn't able to describe it, but it was palpable when there. For example, in Lhasa Tibet, you could almost feel the resistance between the Tibetans and the Chinese. Not a violent resistance, but some sort of metaphysical pushback. In Jerusalem, Gabe once found himself having dinner next to an Israeli and a Palestinian and felt almost a camaraderie between the two. In Paris, romance springs naturally from the air. Gabe believed that this type of magic was like an energy field that made these places unique. Sajama had it. It was more than beauty, it was more than any dramatic natural features, it was more than people or culture or society; it was just something awesome, something sublime. If he coupled Sajama's natural landscape with the church at Curahuara de Carangas, he had his new favorite place on the planet.

That afternoon and the next morning, the brothers drove around the entire peak of Sajama, stopping to take pictures and even finding a small watering hole that was home to hundreds of pink flamingos. *More birds!* Gabe mainly just looked out the windows of the truck, still in awe of the landscape. He thought of all the hassles with the strike that canceled his first trip and the nearly year-long delay in getting into Sajama National Park; the wait was worth it.

• • •

Larry left South America two days later, and Gabe was again on his own in La Paz. But instead of sinking under the dread and feelings of isolation that beset him after his mom and aunt had left in the fall, his spirit held light and his attitude was positive. His brother had seen a part of the world he couldn't have found on a map four years before, and the trip had brought them closer, which was invaluable.

At that point, Gabe still fell into believing he had accomplished nothing much with the nonprofit, and most days he still felt like a failure. But then he remembered that if all the pain and suffering of his year in Bolivia had brought him closer to his family, then maybe the endeavor had been worth it; maybe that was the payoff, the real reason for this journey.

Gabe stared at the calendar. He now had only three weeks until his year in Bolivia was going to end. He counted the days. But as it turned out once again, life didn't follow the plan. He was going to have to wait just a little while longer before making his way back to the US.

CHAPTER TWENTY-FOUR
MOVING DIRT

When his brother left, Gabe had only a couple of weeks left before flying home to Colorado on June 15, exactly one year to the day after he had arrived in Bolivia. He liked the synergy. Once again, he was planning, just like he had twelve months earlier: finding a place to live, getting his addresses updated, canceling all the personal utilities and accounts he had in Bolivia. Of course, coming back to the US was easier than entering Bolivia, but all these activities were bittersweet, nonetheless. His year of setting up operations for Pidola was coming to an end, just not the end he had hoped for. But he could congratulate himself for many things. At the very least, Pidola was now able to manage projects from Colorado due to the operations he had established. He had a new personal best with altitude. He'd offered new experiences to his family and was closer to his brother. He'd survived. His Spanish, well, still a work in progress.

One of the steps he took when moving *to* Bolivia was establishing a connection in the US State Department. Many people who travel internationally register with the State Department, just in case there's an emergency—civil unrest, injury or sickness, a pandemic, whatever. Everyone has their opinions about the US government, but Gabe's experience was that whenever he worked with the State Department, they had his back. Before he left Colorado for Bolivia, they knew he was coming.

He had the chance to meet with people who worked at the State Department in Tel Aviv back in 2012 and was impressed with both public and private sector work they were doing in Israel. After landing in La Paz in June 2018 and getting himself situated, he made connections with various people at the embassy there. The State Department had been in Bolivia for decades, and he figured they could have some connections in-country that would help Pidola's projects. Plus, if he *did* have an emergency, it would be nice to know people on a personal level that may be able to help out.

The American embassy was located in a massive fortress right in downtown La Paz; ten stories high, it was a big tan cube of a building surrounded by twelve-foot walls and barbed wire. It was as secure a place as could be—exponentially more secure than Bolivia's presidential residence just three blocks away. Despite the imposing building, the State Department's presence in Bolivia was a shell of its former self, especially after Evo Morales took office. Since the relationship between the two countries was fractured, there weren't as many US diplomats as in the pre-Evo era.

Initially, Gabe visited the US Embassy for general tasks: visa application, paperwork from the States that needed to be notarized, passport stuff, and other minor items. Later, and as he was introduced to other people at the embassy, he would visit to talk about Pidola's work and how the State Department could assist. It was an interesting relationship, especially since he was at times brokering conversations between the two governments.

Some of the diplomats' work at the State Department focused on economic development, cultural development, and sometimes just general consular activities. Gabe tried to meet anyone and everyone, since he never knew when an opportunity would arise that would help raise funds for projects. In fact, his main goal in networking at the embassy was to develop relationships with potential donors so Pidola could build and launch more projects. Embassy contacts were nice to have, but funds were necessary to implement the work.

As Gabe met more people, the more he understood that the US State Department was still active in Bolivian communities, and in many different ways. He was initially invited to a small event in Zona Sur in southern La Paz where they were announcing some new business relationships in the city. Then, he received an invitation to a July 4 party in Santa Cruz, which was about a two-hour plane ride east of La Paz, back in the heat and humidity of the Amazon River Basin. Amazingly, the invitation included the offer for Pidola to be a sponsor there. Gabe couldn't believe what he was reading. He was almost enthusiastic.

Many of the events the State Department hosted allowed local companies to sponsor in order to promote their businesses. Pidola would be the smallest sponsor *by far*. It was amazing that this mom-and-pop nonprofit would be a sponsor of the embassy's event celebrating the fiftieth anniversary of the Apollo moon landing. It was an ideal situation to promote Pidola's work, build some awareness, expand networks, and most importantly, develop financial support. In theory, Gabe could meet folks from local companies with war chests full of cash, good citizens looking to help their Bolivian neighbors.

However, the event was to take place on June 30, two weeks *after* his already scheduled flight home. So, what if Gabe stayed just a little while longer. He had come to Bolivia for a reason, to push forward good work. Could he really pass up this opportunity to promote

Pidola's efforts? What if he missed the chance to find a significant donor. *I made it this far. I can surely make it a couple more weeks.*

He changed his flight back to Colorado… to July 6.

So planning started. It was early June, and he was easily the last sponsor to register for the event; all others had their act together. The scrambling also started … booking flights to and from Santa Cruz, ordering a standing banner with Pidola's name and logo on it, reserving a hotel room, coordinating schedules with the State Department, and even ordering more business cards. He had hoped to get Lidy there as well, but she couldn't join him. He thought, *Ah, it's a State Department event, I should be okay not knowing much Spanish.*

As with most of his assumptions in South America, he couldn't have been more wrong.

His main point of contact within the State Department also invited him to a side event happening the day before the celebration in Santa Cruz. One of the embassy's partnerships was with Habitat for Humanity working to build bathrooms that would be part of newly developed houses on the outskirts of Santa Cruz. The group attending, which included people from the embassy and representatives from the Bolivian government, also included all event sponsors. Possibly another great networking opportunity.

• • •

On June 29 Gabe flew into Santa Cruz. The hotel where he was staying was the location for the celebration the following day, which was very convenient. Whereas La Paz was the administrative capital of Bolivia, Santa Cruz was the unofficial economic capital. Many Bolivian-based companies were headquartered there.

Settled on the fringes of the Amazon River Basin, Santa Cruz was downright tropical. To Gabe, it had the feel of Miami without the beach. As he drove in from the airport to the hotel, Gabe scanned the area for birds and spotted a half-dozen he could now identify.

The following day, in the lobby he ran into some of the embassy folks also staying at the hotel, and together, they headed to the Habitat for Humanity event. There were about a dozen people in a small sprinter van, but Gabe was the only event sponsor; the rest were embassy employees. It was nice to meet more people from the State Department, and it was a plus to be able to speak English with people from all over the US.

That day, Gabe thought that maybe he could be stationed abroad as a diplomat for the United States. Throughout his time in Bolivia, he had gained such an appreciation for the US that he had become prouder to be American. Yes, his home country had lots of problems, and plenty of political turmoil was just ahead. But comparatively? Gabe knew that some Americans who feel that way get the call to serve in the military. He was getting that same call to work at the State Department.

It was only a twenty-minute ride to the destination, an open field in the suburbs of Santa Cruz. It was about midday, and the heat and humidity were *pumping*. A few clouds blocked the sun, but not enough to give cover and to prevent the team from being utterly baked. Gabe was nonetheless energetic, since it had been well over a year since he had done some good old-fashioned grunt labor.

Participating groups congregated under a large event tent in the middle of the field; they had at least some cover. There was nothing in any direction for at least a half mile except for the foundations of a dozen homes being developed adjacent to the tent. There were probably a hundred people in total helping with this project, folks from Habitat for Humanity, the local press, and the construction crew that helped guide this group in developing new bathrooms—a good thing since probably no one in this group had the skills to work on these sites unsupervised. Groups of six headed to the foundations of future home sites.

Gabe didn't know anyone in his group, which was nothing new at that point. After traveling around Bolivia for almost a year, one more group of unfamiliar faces wasn't a concern. The construction crew broke us into smaller groups of three each and gave instructions. One group would lay bricks and vertically extend the foundation and the other—Gabe's group—would build the bathroom. *Bathroom* was a loose term. They were building a squat toilet, essentially digging an eight-foot deep and five-foot-wide pit. Moving more dirt.

For Gabe, manual labor was always therapeutic. Larry and their dad were both mechanics and his brother Randy worked on sheet metal for helicopters. None of them were afraid of a little hard work. However, despite being in great shape from climbing, Gabe quickly discovered that digging and moving dirt required a different kind of physical fitness. Still, he jumped into the work whole-heartedly.

Given that he was one of the only sponsors, Gabe wanted to make a good impression, especially because there could be potential donors in the group. In his mind, a donor would think, *Damn, did you see the dude from Pidola move all that dirt? He's worthy of our money.* Of course, even if that didn't happen, he still wanted to put in a solid day of work to help a family get into their new home. The team gave him a shovel, and he started digging.

As usual, he was the only person in the group who didn't speak Spanish, but most of the communication was non-verbal. There he was with two short Bolivian men working in the pit for the first hour. The three shoveled dirt to the side and made small piles around them. But once the pit got too deep to lift and throw the dirt out a bucket system was started to lift dirt from the hole. And with that new system, only one person could be digging at a time. Gabe stayed in the pit for the next three hours, digging, hauling up the buckets, and sweating profusely since he wasn't used to the humidity. No piece of clothing was dry. He could now envision potential donors saying, *Damn, did you see how disgusting the dude from Pidola was? I'm not going near him to give him money.*

Gabe never shied away from a bit of hard work; he actually quite enjoyed it. Clear results, and he would surely pay for it later that day with severe muscle cramps.

There was an added highlight to participating in the Habitat for Humanity event; Gabe got to meet the charge *d'affaires* stationed in Bolivia. He was from Mount Airy, a small neighborhood in Philadelphia. It was nice to not have to bumble through a Spanish conversation, plus they talked about Philly sports for close to forty-five minutes. Gabe was sure he appreciated the conversation as well, since so many of the embassy staff were from different parts of the country and had their different sports-team loyalties.

The labor came to a halt mid-afternoon. The three men on Gabe's team all looked at their hole and shook hands at a job well done. They'd completed the work they were tasked with, just like the handful of other groups had. Gabe felt good about the accomplishment, but he also felt like he had when coming off Illimani—totally shredded. He went back to the hotel, grabbed some dinner, and slept for twelve hours.

• • •

Gabe woke up sore beyond belief. And not just the general, *I put in a good workout* sore, but so sore that it hurt to breathe. He'd overdone it and was paying for it. Fortunately, he had hours to loosen and limber up before the event that evening.

The hotel had a huge atrium that went all the way to the roof, twenty floors above. Gabe strolled through it ahead of time to get the lay of the land. It was set up with a podium, chairs, tables for light hors d'oeuvres and drinks, banners for the sponsors and donors, Pidola's, too, and American flags all over the place. That last seemed slightly odd in the middle of South America, but he appreciated it, nonetheless.

Gabe suited up, thankful that the building had air conditioning. With a stack of business cards in his pocket, he made his way to the ground floor to work the room. Since he already knew a few people from the Habitat for Humanity event, he wasn't too nervous or anxious. Then, as he quickly started to make the rounds in the room, he realized that most conversations were in Spanish. Introducing himself and moving immediately to a funding ask probably wouldn't be the best approach to break the ice, but his vocabulary was limited. He definitely missed having an interpreter. This celebration was quickly becoming a microcosm of his entire year in Bolivia, so much promise but an inability to deliver.

Disheartened, he attempted to rally, thinking *I didn't get dressed up for nothing.* But over the next three hours, outside of the people he had already met from the embassy, he spoke to exactly two people, a professor from Santa Cruz University and a significant other of one of the embassy employees. On top of it all, Pidola's banner was in the back corner of the atrium, getting very little attention or foot traffic—the by-product of being the last and smallest sponsor of the event. *Disaster.*

There were about two hundred people at the celebration event, most likely a successful event for the State Department. The *chargé d'affaires* he'd talked sports with the day before addressed the crowd for about ten minutes. Gabe was proud of his fellow Philadelphian at the podium, ripping through Spanish, holding the audience's attention. But that sense of pride quickly evaporated once he concluded his remarks and Gabe realized that he couldn't have spoken for two minutes in Spanish.

He called it an evening and went back to his room. Looking down from outside his door at the group below, everyone seemed to be having a wonderful time. He simply wasn't cut out for this type of event. That old familiar inner voice was at it. *You've failed again.*

Alone and disappointed, he resolved to focus on something more positive. His time in this country was quickly coming to an end. He had one more journey before heading back to the States—a visit to Raul, their birding guide from Rurre, and then just one week before being back on American soil.

CHAPTER TWENTY-FIVE
BREAKFAST PIRANHA

Even though Gabe had flown into Rurrenabaque with his brother Larry just a couple months earlier, he was still in awe when the plane began its descent for landing. The environments in Bolivia were just so dramatically different but almost always raw, untamed. Everything below—the snakes, spiders, jaguars, and unnamed other threats—all scared the hell out of him.

Between waves of nausea from the descent and looking down at the green canopy of trees, he had thought, *What if I got lost in there?* Even though he'd had *some* survival training, it was limited and untested, plus only for mountainous terrain. He couldn't imagine getting lost in these forests. Movies of people running through the jungle from maniacs or predators were unrealistic. *In the real jungle, you can't run, it's way too dense. I'd only last about an hour down there . . . if that.*

After collecting his bag, Gabe used a half-bottle of bug spray to ward off mosquitos and waited for his ride.

When Larry and Gabe first visited Rurre, Gabe spoke to Raul a number of times about the work he was doing in Bolivia, and Raul was curious about the projects. Even though Pidola's efforts were being scoped and completed in other areas of the country—Potosi, Cochabamba, Santa Cruz— Raul knew that the initiatives were needed in his home state of Beni, too. When they'd parted, Gabe promised to reach out and keep the conversations going. After several texts and phone calls, here he was, back in Raul's neighborhood and planning to visit various communities who needed what Pidola could bring.

The first night at the hotel, Gabe barely slept. He was dealing with the usual excitement and anxiety before going to new communities to determine if they'd be a good candidate. Plus, the locations outside of Rurre were unique; the two that he would be visiting were accessible only by boat. It would not be a simple crossing of the small river near San Jose de la Angosta, but a five-and-a-half-hour ride, and hardly a pleasure excursion. There were no roads to these villages, and there was definitely no major infrastructure connecting them to the outside world. They would be some of the most remote places Gabe had ever been, or likely would ever visit. The more remote a location, the greater the chance of encountering a dangerous situation.

La Paz taxi drivers had been aloof and even rude to outsiders mostly because they were wary of the intruders' intentions. The same with people on the streets and in the shops, fueling Gabe's paranoia. Even a garden-variety mugging would put him in a very compromised situation, since the closest person he knew other than Raul was two hundred and fifty miles away. There was no cell phone reception, either so if anything happened on this trip, he was very much on his own.

The day started early—they'd be traveling for twelve hours. Gabe met Raul at his small office in the middle of town and they walked down the street to the docks on the Beni. "Docks" was, like many other terms in Bolivia, a loose term. Boats were propped up against the shoreline waiting to transfer people and products. Boats ferried everything from fruits, meats, vegetables, and medicines to hundreds of people living up and down the river. The docks were active each morning with everyone getting all their affairs in order and ready for the day's travel.

Dozens of boats surrounded Gabe and Raul's, all preparing to depart. The craft they were to board was more like a canoe than a riverboat—maybe thirty feet long and a few feet wide, with a small outboard motor. Raul and Gabe plus a few other people were being taken up the river, everyone to be dropped off at various points. It was a common practice for boatmen to give people rides to their villages; most rides would only cost a Boliviano or two.

The boat departed from Rurre at six that morning and started upriver—the direction of La Paz. It was cloudy, which was a blessing since the humidity must have been two hundred percent, and Gabe was wearing thin pants and a light jacket. Long pants and sleeves were an absolute must, no matter how uncomfortable you became. Total annihilation by mosquitos and subsequent malaria are real dangers, not imagined.

You're never comfortable in Bolivia.

• • •

The community of Carmen Florida was just thirty minutes upriver. The boat docked on the south side of the river and Gabe and Raul stepped onto a beach that was only a few meters wide. Raul waved down a gentleman he recognized, and they had their familiar Bolivian greeting of a handshake, a hug, and a second handshake. Gabe of course butchered his greeting. The three of them then took a sandy trail through plantain groves, and within fifteen minutes Gabe wished that the pants and jacket were unnecessary; sweat was pouring off him. Even after the days in the bludgeoning humidity of Santa Cruz, he was not used to the tropical environment of Rurre.

They wound down the forested path and entered the village, another with only a handful of buildings, most of which were designed for communal purposes. The middle of the village had a large field for various activities, primarily soccer games. To the right of the field from where they were standing, immediately off the trail, was an open-air community pavilion similar to those in local parks in the States. Gabe introduced himself to the local community leaders and held a few brief conversations with the help of Raul as interpreter.

Every time Gabe visited a local community, he brought gifts, and today was no different. He always had either school supplies or soccer balls or both—things primarily for the children. If nothing else, it started off his relationship with community leaders on the right foot.

For Carmen Florida, Gabe brought school supplies since they took up less room on the boat. This made him instantly popular with the local schoolchildren, especially since he was the odd foreigner visiting their village. Even after more than twelve months in Bolivia, and almost five years since his first trip to Monte Rancho, he still enjoyed the children's reaction to seeing him—and his beard—for the first time. The kids were always curious and always welcoming—eventually.

For the initial fifteen minutes of the meeting, Gabe spoke to the local leaders under the pavilion. He passed out some of the usual materials and information, and supplemented the Pidola one-pager with his Spanish description of the goals and intentions of the projects. Raul was interpreting and the initial reaction from the community leaders was positive. Most meetings involved sharing project ideas first, then the community presenting back their needs for the village, mainly surrounding their lack of resources.

Every village Gabe had visited over the years had its own individual characteristics. The leaders of Carmen Florida surprised him with a couple of their requests; first, they would need electricity in the village. They were not connected to the power grid and infrastructure, which wasn't surprising since they were fairly remote and difficult to reach. Carmen Florida was in a unique position from a geographical standpoint, though. The Beni River was the border between two of the nine states of Bolivia—Beni and La Paz. The villagers of Carmen Florida in Beni could see their sister villages in La Paz across the river. Since they were in different states, they had different government entities handling their infrastructure needs and development. The villages on the La Paz side of the Beni River were connected to the power grid, so those villages had electricity. Every night, the communities on the Beni side could look across the river and see their neighbors on the La Paz side with their lights on. Gabe thought, *How heartbreaking to see your neighbors with lights on each night, and your community, family, and friends without such a basic resource.*

The second surprise was that after initial conversations the community leaders of Carmen Florida asked Gabe to leave the pavilion—not permanently, fortunately—to give them time to discuss the proposal and potential subsequent projects. Gabe obliged.

Typically, a response back from the village leaders was immediate, but not in Carmen Florida. For a half hour, Gabe walked alone in circles around the grass field in the middle of the village, a stranger in a strange land. He was confident the community would be receptive, so he spent this time taking in the surroundings, like the chickens that roamed outside of the field perimeter. He shot photos of the infrastructure that did exist to determine potential areas for solar panels, and he smiled and waved to the few children who were not with their parents under the pavilion. Sweat ran down his back.

How did I end up here?

The familiar question reared its head, now making him shake his head and chuckle.

Finally, Raul asked him to return to the pavilion, which felt a little like a criminal returning to the courtroom, where the jury was going to read a verdict. The good news was that no matter what, he wasn't going to be thrown in jail. Even better, the community of Carmen Florida would be thrilled to continue conversations about installing renewable energy and internet service within their village.

Hugs and botched handshakes ensued, and it was now time for them to welcome their guests properly. As with every village meeting, the hospitality was almost overwhelming. The villagers served a full meal.

Each location also had its own cuisine—meals that Gabe couldn't get anywhere else. Most places had chicken; other places like Pampa Jasi had goat. Amid acres of plantain trees, Gabe was hardly surprised to see those being served. There was also seasoned rice and potatoes, and a nice change of pace—fish. They lived right on the river, so it made sense. That was a treat, as eating canned soup, baked goods and cereal for the last six months had grown unbearable. Gabe asked Raul what kind of fish it was. He was anticipating a reply of some type of trout, bass, maybe catfish.

"Pirana," Raul said, forgetting to translate the word into English.

Gabe thought to himself for the thousandth time in Bolivia that he'd heard something incorrectly. Then Raul saw the confusion on Gabe's face and was himself confused. The word really didn't need much translating. *Yes, it was piranha.*

Gabe had the same reaction he would have had being offered rattlesnake or crocodile.

There was absolutely no way that he *wasn't* going to eat the meal this community was offering, since it would undoubtedly offend the hosts. So, he dug in. "This is good," Gabe thought. *I'd definitely recommend it.*

If you've never eaten piranha, and you have the opportunity, please take it. Sure, it's a bit boney and it takes effort to get good chunks of meat. But damn, if it's prepared as well as in Carmen Florida, it's a wonderful treat—even at nine in the morning.

• • •

After about an hour of eating and conversation it was time to part ways so they could move on to the next destination, Torewa. Raul and Gabe said their goodbyes to the people of Carmen Florida and walked back through the plantain trees and down to the boat that was taking them further upriver. They stepped on board and got as comfortable as possible for the next leg—a four-hour ride.

They passed through the gorgeous, forested ridge that the Beni River split in half and entered a vast plain of jungle that spanned dozens if not hundreds of miles in each direction. The proper beginning of the Andes mountains was in the very far distance. The area felt almost untouched by humans—otherworldly, or so ancient that a dinosaur's head might emerge from the jungle canopy. Raul and the passengers chatted about the strange guy on the boat—Gabe—and what he was doing in this part of the country. With Raul's help, Gabe joined the discussions about the upcoming federal and local elections.

The scenery was beautiful for the entire forty-mile trip, the river wide and majestic and the jungle green and lush, dramatic with gray and dark blue clouds as a backdrop. Still, the farther they went upriver, the more anxious Gabe became. Deep down he felt safe being with Raul, but there was always risk involved. They were heading to a place he felt very few outsiders—if any—had ever visited, a place where the indigenous may never have encountered Westerners.

What will happen to me if something happens to Raul? If I have to, will I be able to get back to Rurre just walking the banks of the river? Would I even make it? What would happen if the boat just sank?

It was always possible that Gabe put too much faith into people that he barely knew—or didn't know at all.

After four hours, endless anxious thoughts, and an increasingly sore butt, Gabe realized they had finally made it to the stopping point for Torewa. They unloaded some packages destined for the village and then entered the jungle for a thirty-minute walk. The trail into Torewa was different from that into Carmen Florida in that it was through thick forests, not groves of plantains. The palm trees weren't tall, so they received a decent amount of light from above. But stepping ten feet to either side of the trail could put you at risk of getting lost. The intensity of insects just off the path was beyond belief, just a wall of bugs.

Gabe was again drenched in sweat as they entered the village of Torewa, which was basically a clearing. One building was the pavilion, and another had previously been used as a schoolhouse and was dilapidated. Raul and Gabe entered the pavilion, where villagers sporadically came to greet them. Just as in Carmen Florida, Gabe made his presentation and with Raul's help engaged in conversations. He was encouraged. They seemed genuinely interested in what Pidola could offer, and they celebrated with everyone over a meal. Everyone was gracious, welcoming, and hospitable.

And just like all the other villages that Gabe had visited, Torewa was unique. The meal consisted of crackers. Gabe very much appreciated any food offered, whether it be chicken, soup, goat, or piranha. Crackers were also fine. That wasn't what caused Gabe's heart to sink. The issue was that these eighty or so people had nothing more to offer than crackers. Knowing how hospitable Bolivians are, Gabe imagined how much pain the situation must have caused them. Bolivians want to make visitors feel at home and comfortable, and the people of Torewa made that attempt as best they could. They succeeded more than they could know. Gabe felt very much at home, even though his heart was heavy seeing their conditions.

The second unique characteristic in Torewa was the lack of a church. It was the first time that Gabe had been to a community that didn't have one, or at least some sort of building that served as one. For hundreds of years, missionaries scattered themselves all over South America to spread the gospel of Christianity. About ninety-five percent of Bolivians practice Christianity or Catholicism, so a church was central to a community. The lack of a church in Torewa caught him by surprise. Maybe his instinct was correct; maybe Gabe was the first Westerner to visit this village. Naturally, some of the villagers in Torewa had *seen* foreigners when they went into Rurre, the closest town, but it was possible that no other Westerner traveled the Beni River and got off at this point, at least not recently. If so, Gabe truly was an ambassador for the West to this group of eighty or so people.

For most of Gabe's life, he had longed to do something no one else had. However minor the impact of his visit to Torewa, it fit that category. No amount of money could buy this sort of experience, and he was humbled and grateful that his stumbling through the universe brought him there, to a remote corner of a beautiful country where he was welcomed wholeheartedly by people whose generosity—sharing the very little they had to eat—he would never forget.

• • •

Project approved, Raul and Gabe said their goodbyes and headed back to the riverboat and subsequently back to Rurre. It had turned into a successful day; both communities were receptive, and more, Gabe had made memories that would last him the rest of his life.

They pushed the boat back into the water and started downriver; Raul and Gabe were on the boat, but two other passengers were also looking for rides back into town. As they made their way east, the clouds started to thicken, and Gabe realized that they were going to get drenched by rain. The four of the passengers hunkered down, and Gabe was overcome with total exhaustion. This fatigue wasn't your average Friday-afternoon-after-a-long-week tiredness, or even being worn out after climbing a mountain or digging a squat toilet. It was a kind of pure exhaustion that he had never experienced before. After thirteen months—or more like almost a half-decade of getting things organized and being constantly prepared—his mind and body started to shut down. The effects of his persistence, grit, and perseverance that had taken him all the way to Torewa descended on him.

He'd finished. He'd done it. He could finally breathe out.

Their two fellow passengers lay down with their feet toward the back of the boat and their heads behind some packages they were taking into town. When the rain started, the two guys were perfectly situated so that they could sleep the whole way, their heads staying dry; they knew the tricks of traveling through the jungle by water. From a lifetime of taking this route, they knew how to get comfortable and make the best of the time. Given how tired Gabe was, he decided to join them. He was as present as his mom on Lake Titicaca, as joyful as his brother Larry beaming at a nunbird.

Before he fell asleep, Gabe was overwhelmed with gratitude for nothing more than the experiences of a day like that one. For the first time since hitting rock bottom in December, he was thankful to be alive.

CHAPTER TWENTY-SIX
MOVING UP NORTH

A couple of days later, Gabe was sitting in his nearly empty apartment back in La Paz. At around eight that night, he was getting ready to grab a taxi to head to the airport up in El Alto. He was entering the last few hours of living in Bolivia, and all his bags were packed with what he had remaining in the country. His belongings now fit in three large backpacks.

Over forty years of my life in those bags. Surreal.

As was always the case with flights that departed in the middle of the night, Gabe left a few hours early to go to the airport. With mixed emotions, he took a look around the apartment for one last time. Now, he was disappointed that he was leaving such a great place and foregoing more opportunities to make an impact. He was also relieved; the worst anguish he'd ever experienced was being put behind him. And finally, there was a bit of excitement as well, as anyone would feel when starting an unknown chapter of life.

When he turned the lights off, the apartment felt emptier than it had ever been, perhaps as a metaphor for what had happened inside him during those thirteen months. The lights from the street lit up the yellow walls, and the space almost glowed. As cold and unwelcoming the apartment had been when he first arrived, it now seemed almost cozy and warm. He left the keys on the floor and closed the door behind him for the final time.

Carrying his bags through the streets of La Paz, Gabe nearly laughed out loud at the thought; *What if I finally got mugged of all my stuff on my last trip to the airport?* He was numb to the idea since he really had nothing of any great importance or value in those bags; the joke would be on the thief. Also, he knew now that most things were completely out of his control.

It was a cool evening, the type of clear weather that enhances all of your senses. On the way to the Teleferico station where he could catch a taxi, he inhaled the aromas emerging from the restaurants he passed and heard the chatter in Spanish of late-night diners. He felt the weight of his bags and the pavement under his feet. His skin tingled with awareness of the crisp dry air.

He flagged down a cab and filled the trunk and backseat with his bags. As they drove up the winding streets of La Paz, he looked back down the valley that cupped the city, and what he saw astounded him. Seeing the city lights below him was like looking down on the stars. Even after a year of being there, he was amazed at how stunning the city of La Paz was at night. He didn't know of any other city in the world that offered that sort of view. La Paz, just like all the villages he visited that year, had unique traits and characteristics that he would now carry with him wherever he went.

That ride offered him for the first time a chance to reflect on the trip to Rurre a few days before. All of the planning and logistics of moving home to another continent were complete, and his mind was clear to think about some of the most recent events. Life became simple again. He breathed deeply and allowed himself to feel pride. Yes, he was proud of having been an ambassador to people who had never before met anyone from the Western world.

As he continued to reflect, he realized he'd also been an ambassador for many other things. He represented the United States to these people as surely as did any American ambassador. But he was also an ambassador for Colorado. He was also an ambassador for Denver. It struck him that in fact he was an ambassador for everyone and everything that contributed to who he was: his family, his friends, his culture, his schools, and universities. For all the people who had ever cared about him, he humbly represented them.

What am I, after all, but a reflection of all the impacts you all have instilled in me over the more than forty years of my life?

He realized on the trip back to Colorado that he needed to keep this mindset and reflect on it on a day-to-day basis. Meeting the community of Torewa was a once in a lifetime experience, a turning point teaching him that at any given moment, he now mirrored the people who cared about him. He was their ambassador to the world around him. He didn't know if he'd ever again see the people he met or go to the places he had visited. Through the confusion of memories and emotions, gratitude emerged as the most dominant impression from everything he went through. The good, and maybe even more importantly, the bad, all happened for a reason. Yes, there's magic at the bottom.

Starting his new chapter, he expected that he would learn why all this had happened to him; the reason. He'd been through the hardest part, and as much as he was right there in the moment, he also couldn't wait to start the process of rebuilding.

POSTFACE

I started this book on my birthday, 2019, at the Alexander Cafe near Abaroa Plaza, and finished it at OCF, a small coffee shop in Philadelphia. It took me over two thousand days to develop and write what's in your hands today. And it couldn't have taken one minute less; the last ten pages alone took over two years to develop. Sure, the stories themselves were not hard to write; I mean, I already knew them, because I lived them. When I began to write, everything was just notes to preserve my memories and thoughts.

And to be honest, I was scared to death to make all of this public. What would my family and friends think of me? How would this affect my career? Would this negatively affect people around me? How would this affect my love life? (Tongue in cheek, that last question wasn't really a concern. It can't get any worse). I simply took baby steps to get myself started.

During that car ride my last night in La Paz, back to the airport in El Alto, I remember thinking, *It's going to take the rest of my life to really understand and comprehend all that I went through over the thirteen months*. All of the ups, but mainly the downs. And what caused me to get there, to hit bottom? But I wasn't feeling pressure to get to that understanding, I had the rest of my life to dig into the details. As it turned out, it took about four years.

• • •

So, I came home, back to Colorado. And once again, just like after my very first trip back in 2015, life fell into place just like it did before I left. It was almost like I had never left. I was seeing family, hanging out with friends, doing all the things that I had done before the move. Working full-time. Climbing. Hiking. And during those first weeks and months after my return, I really didn't feel anything at all. No emotions were stirred. Again, like I never experienced South America.

Then, after twelve months...

I can remember it like it was yesterday. It was a Thursday in mid-June 2020. Just your garden-variety afternoon where I was coming back from Denver to my place in Silverthorne, about seventy miles west of the city, which I'd moved into late the previous year.

Something triggered a release of emotions. I had a strong, cathartic response, similar to what I experienced when I was sitting in my car in early 2016 outside of the YMCA down in Golden. It was a full release like I had experienced before, but little did I know that it was just the initial crack in the dam. And that I was about to break wide open.

Then the following day, I had another breakdown that was the same as the one the day before. And then later that day, another one. And then another.

Then more of the same the following day. Two, three, four complete breakdowns. Multiple breakdowns each and every day. And not just for a few minutes, but for about thirty minutes at a time. Some even for an hour. Breakdowns that were so intense that I would lose track of time. I would find clothing all around me that I hadn't been wearing: winter gloves, socks, jackets, etc. These breakdowns would be so severe that my entire abdomen would seize up, or I would pop a blood vessel in my eye. Massive headaches would frequently follow.

This went on, every day for three months straight. I was either going into a breakdown, having one, or coming out of one. I was amazed that I was even able to hold onto my job. Looking back now, I guess I was having some sort of nervous breakdown. But I wasn't worried about it, since I figured it was just Bolivia coming up and out. At least initially.

However, it continued. After that second month, I started to get concerned. Really concerned. Was I losing my mind? Should I go to the hospital? Should I have myself committed? I believed it was just a release of all that I had experienced, but I was getting nervous, nonetheless.

Just when I was sure I was losing my mind, thankfully the breakdowns started to lessen. Maybe just a couple a day, then down to one a day. Then, I was able to go a full day without any tears. I was coming out of it, relieved. It was then, when I was able to have a clearer mind, I started to realize that it wasn't just Bolivia that was being released with these breakdowns. It was my entire life. All of the negativity, all of the profound loneliness, all of the extreme sorrow and isolation. All of the self-loathing, negativity, and resentments against those who had what I *thought* I wanted. A breaking down of all of the walls and armor I had built up over the years and years of disappointment and sadness. It all came up and out. My metaphysical life was being released through these breakdowns.

• • •

As the breakdowns became fewer and fewer, I started the process of planning a trip back to Bolivia, this time just for a climb. A few friends of mine asked me to help them plan, and participate in, climbing Illampu. The same high peak I wondered if I'd ever climb when my mom, aunt and I were taking a boat across Lake Titicaca.

As you understand better now, training was required for this high peak. There were six trailheads within a quarter mile of my condo. Almost ideal conditions for training, especially since I was again living above ten thousand feet. So, the training began in earnest.

Just like eighteen months before when I trained for Illimani, I would load my seventy-liter backpack with forty pounds of sand to mimic carrying a larger load. I walked the neighborhood streets and trails to get back into climbing shape. The neighbors would always give me a wry look. The neighborhood dogs mostly left me alone.

The trip would ultimately never happen since this was right about the time of the covid-19 pandemic and the almost global lockdown. Bolivia was no different since they were not allowing anyone in or out of the country unless they had permission from the government. We indefinitely postponed our trip.

But during the months of training for Illampu, there wasn't just a physical transformation that happened. There was a cognitive one as well.

My mind was clearer, and I had recognized that all of those breakdowns released pain and suffering that I kept deep down, probably for most of my adult life. But it wasn't just that specific insight; my thoughts were clearer for just about everything.

When I was working, the thoughts and ideas came more quickly, more easily. The conversations I was having were deeper, richer. My relationships began to be more authentic. My entire life became more real. I couldn't explain it, nor can I fully explain it today, but the weeks and months of emotional release also brought me a cognitive change. I was seeing things in a different light. A changed perspective.

In early fall 2020, I was also hit with another proverbial sack of potatoes. A friend of mine was having a tough go of it, and we decided to get out for a hike one Saturday morning. On the side of Mount Aetna near Monarch Pass, we were having a glorious day. Engaged in good conversations, we were enjoying the snowpack with crampons on, axes in hand. And at about thirteen thousand five hundred feet, that sack fell from the sky. At forty-one years old, my entire life changed in an instant once again. I knew with total confidence, and with some relief, that it became abundantly clear about *where* I needed to be; it was time for me to move back East to Philadelphia. There was nothing left to do, no place else to go, no one else to be. My time in Colorado had come to an end. That instantly, I knew I needed to be closer to my family.

• • •

I moved back to Philadelphia on October 15, 2020. I had been in Colorado for exactly ten years and five days. Looking back on my time out West, I feel that I squeezed every last drop out of that experience. Climbing mountains, grad school, establishing Pidola, building my career, circumnavigating the globe, living abroad. I don't think that I could have gotten more out of that decade. But when I finally got settled back in Philadelphia, the big questions *still* had to be answered. What have I learned from all of this? And how did I get myself into such a bad mental state?

Even though I had those months of breakdowns and breakthroughs, I knew that I would need to complete some intense therapy. Given that I was in such a bad frame of mind in late 2018 and early 2019, I had to understand why I got there in the first place, why I was there for so long, and how to as best as possible prevent myself from going into those dark places in the future. I had made promises to my closest friends that I'd put in the work and ensure I was healing.

For over three years, I hunkered down to look inside. I had heard about Buddhist monks and practitioners heading into the mountains and caves to meditate for years to better understand themselves. Of course, I wasn't in an actual cave, but I look on those first years back in Philadelphia as spending time in my own cave, gaining an understanding of who I am, who I was, what has caused my mental health crises, and how to make improvements to ensure I'm living my best life for the next thirty-to-forty years. I needed to take a serious look inside.

I spoke to therapists, psychologists, and psychtraumatologists. I had conversations with Buddhists, priests, and spiritual advisers. And I read: Frankl, Warburton, Tolle, Thich Nhat Hanh, Tedeschi, Chodron. Sartre, Kant, Singer, Peirce. I became a sponge absorbing information so I could better comprehend these experiences. And I walked, thought, and spent almost every day meditating on my couch cushions. Hundreds, if not for thousands of hours. At the end of the day, self-reflection and analysis helped get me to where I am today.

I initially thought that my entire adult life was essentially a paradox, that everything that I wanted ended up being right where I left it initially in Philadelphia, that I had to leave in order to realize I never had to leave. But, after additional analysis, that wasn't correct. I *did* have to leave to find the bottom, the worst and ugliest form of myself. And now I know what that looks like. How that situation feels, how to recognize it. And to understand that there's magic at the bottom. I can live life knowing what my bottom looks and feels like. Finding the bottom is so important... maybe almost necessary?

It was thus far the greatest gift to myself, and I can now live with fearless curiosity.

• • •

I also learned that meaning, in *my* life, wasn't about making a big splash in the remote places of Bolivia. It may not even be about having a family and children of my own. And it certainly wasn't about having a big house, flashy car, or a big over-flowing bank account. When I was looking for those things, I was chasing the wrong stuff. I could now throw away life's bingo card. Maybe, moving forward, instead of the big splashes, it was just the small, brief impacts that you can make on a day-to-day basis. Very few people will ever get the opportunity to positively impact hundreds of people with projects like in Pampa Jasi. So it comes down to just helping the people immediately around you. They can surely be your family and friends, but maybe it's also the waiter at a restaurant, your barber, the person you let in ahead of you on the highway. Small impacts can lead to doing a lot of good, especially when you can view life through the lens of compassion; knowing that everyone else is just as broken as I am. Just pay attention to the opportunities, which are *always* there, to make a positive impact.

Looking back at 2018 and 2019, I realize now that when I was at my worst, it was the start of the process of getting stripped down to the bare metal. The studs. And what was being removed was all the conditioning, all the stigma, all the bullshit mental muscle memory that had been building up for almost forty years. Any notion of prejudice or pride and any faux confidence that I had was totally blown away. And that has ultimately allowed me to be more compassionate to not only myself, but to the people around me.

And the new-found knowledge of my worst self may be a wonderful biproduct of understanding of not only what the bottom looks like, and how to best manage before I get there, or if I go back there. Of course, I have anxieties and uncertainties like everyone else. But there's less fear now. I have better knowledge of and tools for handling the worst situations.

And looking back on how I was living, even before South America, it was like I was living life with one arm tied behind my back. I didn't really understand who I was, what made me tick, what my triggers were, and still are, and what was *really* most important to me. The storms came and went, and I never got outside to feel the rock. I never explored my life's dark corners, faced what scares me the most. I never realized that I was just moving around, finding new experiences, doing various things that were just distracting me from putting in the hard work. Now, after all the time and effort, I have felt the rock—my rock.

So when I speak to others, I always try to have them lean into something new, lean into something that scares them. Just take the tiniest of steps; again, no big splash is really needed. The idea is to take a small step, stop, look around, and then, hopefully, realize that that wasn't so bad. You took a step into something that scared you, and you survived. Since that first step wasn't so bad, you take another, and then another. All of a sudden, that "thing" that scared you? You've done it. And then you realize, like me, that you've been living with one arm tied behind your back as well. Fearlessness is a wonderful thing, it's just very difficult to find.

These scary growth opportunities are always around us. Maybe it's something relatively minor like trying a new restaurant, or taking a new route to work, or signing up at the gym. Or maybe it's a significant situation like confronting your boss at work, fighting an illness head-on, or getting out of an unhealthy and toxic relationship. Big or small, it's just that initial step. Take it. Then the world will open up and you'll realize, what else can I accomplish?

• • •

If I'm being honest, I still struggle today. But I'm also proud of how far I've come, and I know I'll have many challenges for the rest of my life, big and small. And I have no fairytale ending. Pidola never became wildly successful. I don't have a family of my own. I still live paycheck to paycheck. I struggle with the feeling of not having enough and the ongoing battle with self-worth. But I'm much more hopeful than I was during my time in South America, much more appreciative of what I have, the people in my life, and who I've become, plus all of the immense good around me. And I have brand new measuring sticks of how to see my life's progress. The duty and responsibility to make the world a better place remains, as strong as ever.

ACKNOWLEDGMENTS

I'd like to send a special thank you to Lisa Paige, who without her guidance and coaching, this book would never have seen the light of day. Thank you, Lisa!

And thanks to Koehler Books for their willingness to take a chance on me.

REFERENCES

Below are websites that can be used for people wanting to learn more about the organizations in this book, looking for mental health resources, or if there is ever a mental health emergency:

- Donna's Law—https://www.donnaslaw.com/
- 988 emergency number
- AFSP—https://afsp.org/chapter/greater-philadelphia
- Crisis Text line—"Hello" to 741741
- National Institute of Mental Health—https://www.nimh.nih.gov/health/topics/suicide-prevention
- SPCC—https://suicidepreventioncolorado.org/
- Food for the Hungry—https://www.fh.org/
- Pidola—https://www.pidola.org/

www.ingramcontent.com/pod-product-compliance
Lightning Source LLC
LaVergne TN
LVHW091543070526
838199LV00002B/178